THE
PERSONNEL OF FAIRYLAND

A. A Witch.   B. A Spirit raised by the Witch.
C. A Friar raising his Imps.   D. A Fairy Ring.
E. A Witch rideing on the Devill through the Aire.
F. An Inchanted Castle.

THE
PERSONNEL
OF FAIRYLAND

A short account of the Fairy People of Great Britain
for those who tell Stories to children

by

K. M. BRIGGS

M.A., D.Phil. (Oxon)

ILLUSTRATED BY JANE MOORE

DETROIT
Singing Tree Press
1971

This is a facsimile reprint of the
1953 edition published in Oxford
by the Alden Press. Reissued by
permission of K. M. Briggs.

Library of Congress Catalog Card Number 70-147084

CONTENTS

TYPES OF FAIRIES

PART ONE

THE FAIRY PEOPLE

CONTENTS

PART TWO

THE TUTELARY FAIRIES

CONTENTS

PART THREE

THE NATURE FAIRIES

STORIES:

PART FOUR

MONSTERS, WITCHES AND GIANTS

STORIES:

ILLUSTRATIONS

By JANE MOORE

Frontispiece From the title page of *Pandaemonium, or The Devil's Cloyster*, by R. Bovet.

Chapter Headings From *De Gentibus Septentrionalibus* by Olaus Magnus, and a Seventeenth-Century *Album Amicorum* in the Bodleian Library.

The stories are decorated with original scraper-board designs by Jane Moore.

PREFATORY NOTES

ANYONE who tries to discover what stories modern children know will be struck by the scrappiness of the folklore offered to them, and the large proportion of the foreign to the native even in their genuine folk stories. A great many of the stories which children are told are not folk stories, nor true to the robust tradition of folklore. They are full of careful and innocuous prettinesses, and offer food for the fancy rather than for the imagination. For folklore the story-tellers seem to go chiefly to foreign sources, and our native sources are curiously neglected. There have been most admirable collections of them, but unfortunately nearly all these are out of print.

This little book cannot pretend to take the place of such collections as Jacobs's, Campbell's or Keightley's, nor even of those admirable little books brought out by the Scott Publishing Library at the beginning of the century. It is an attempt rather to describe the characteristics of British fairies, to warn story-tellers off from what Kipling calls 'that sugar-and-shake-your-head set of imposters' which has been usurping the place of real fairies in the children's magazines for the last thirty years, and to give them some idea where to look for suitable stories to tell. In it I have divided the British fairies into rough groupings — exact classification is inexact in folklore — with a description of the habits and appearance of each type, followed by a few specimen stories. I have tried to tell the stories briefly, so that they may be expanded, but not so briefly as to make them dull as they stand. I know from experience that they are all interesting to children.

I have followed the stories with a list of British fairies, very briefly described, and at the end I have put a few suggestions of sources for stories and books on fairy lore.

The book is not for the student of folklore — he knows it all already — and though I have tried to be as accurate as possible I have not given an exhaustive bibliography and have avoided peppering the pages with references.

Many of our native stories are superior to the foreign parallels, and it is a thousand pities that our children should grow up ignorant of their native traditions.

K. M. Briggs

INTRODUCTION

THE different types of fairy melt into each other so much from place to place, and the name of a fairy in one locality is so often used for quite a different type in another, that it is very difficult to dogmatize about the fairies. But children suffer so much nowadays from weakened and sugary fairies of very remote folk origin that I feel that a short book differentiating our native species and giving a few folk stories about each may be found useful by those grown-up people who have occasion, for one reason or another, to tell fairy stories to their youngers.

The name fairy, which I have used to describe the whole race, is not perhaps so well rooted as some, nor is it one which all country people would think it lucky to use, but whether we choose to derive it from the Persian *Peri* or take it, as it is now generally taken, to be related to the word *Fay*, and so to mean either the country of fays or a state of enchantment, we know at least that it has had its present use from the sixteenth century onwards, and that its meaning is generally understood.

When we look through the modern sophisticated fairy stories we find that the writers most generally fall back on the French tradition, in itself a highly sophisticated one. The writers of the Contes des Fées in the reign of Louis XIV were drawing upon folklore sources, but they gave all their stories a courtly turn. If we look at the English, German or Scandinavian variants of the same story we do not find the elaborate etiquette by which the fairies are governed in the Contes des Fées, nor do we find anywhere else the fairy godmother who plays such a large part in our nursery traditions now. The incident of the offended fairy who has not been invited to the christening occurs only in the French fairy stories. Though it has a venerable foundation in the birth gifts of the Fates and Norns it is something of an anachronism at a Christian ceremony. Most folk fairies would rather be offended by being asked to christenings than by being left out.

It would be impossible, even in the most cursory way, to deal with fairies all over the world, or even all over Europe; so I have confined myself to our native fairies, with an occasional passing mention of a foreigner of the same type. Even of the British fairies I shall probably be found to have left out many that are familiar to some of my readers.

The fairies of these islands may roughly be divided into four main types, each with some sub-divisions.

There are first the Fairy People, as they are seen in their own habitations and tribes. They may be divided for convenience into three groups, though these may well be three aspects of the same people. First there are the Heroic Fairies of human stature, or sometimes rather beyond it. These fairies generally live in a Fairyland removed a little from the common world, often underground or in fairy knolls. Time passes there at a different rate from human time. They revel, dance, hunt and sing like humans, only upon a grander scale. Their perfect type is the O'Shee of Ireland, who are supposed to be the Gods of the Danaans who were conquered in the early Fenian invasions.

Second, there are the small Trooping Fairies, such as the Little People of Cornwall. They have a King and Queen and regular government like the Heroic Fairies, but are generally rather homelier in their habits. They delight in music and dancing and are great friends to cleanliness and order. Some types of the Trooping Fairies are almost wholly benevolent, some are mischievous and thieving and child-stealers.

Third, there are the fairies who live in small family groups. These fairies often borrow human beings as nurses, or put their children to be nursed by humans. They are homely little people, who often have occasion to borrow pots or get their tools mended. 'The Fairy Midwife' gives a good description of them on the one side, and the story of 'The Woman of Peace' on the other.

The second great division is the Tutelary Fairies, or those attached to certain families or houses. These are of two kinds, the solemn and comical. The type of the first which will occur to everyone is the Banshee, a spirit attached to certain families, which will wail terribly before the death of any of its family. The second are the hobgoblins, which either attach themselves to a house and work for the inhabitants, like Brownies, or haunt it with mischievous tricks like the Boggart. These domestic hobgoblins are called by a great variety of names, but their characteristics are pretty constant wherever they live.

The third great division is that of the Nature Fairies, most of them water fairies of seas, rivers, lochs or bogs. Some are kindly disposed, but the greater part are malevolent. These fairies are more nearly allied to the rest of fairyland than one might think. Even the highly domesticated Brownie is often associated with some particular stream, and one large branch of the Welsh Tylwyth Teg live in a fairyland guarded by water. There are not many traces of other Nature Fairies in Britain, nothing that quite corresponds to the German Elle-Women, or wood fairies, but the Cailleach Bheur or Blue Hag, who crops up in the North of England as Black Annis or Gentle Annie is probably a symbolization of winter, and so belongs to a rather different type of Nature Fairies.

The fourth division is into monsters, demons and giants, probably most of them originally Nature Spirits, though some are described as ghosts and some as lost races. Dragons and Worms are the most obvious of the monsters, Barguests, Grants and Black Dogs are the demons. The giants vary from being a race of monsters to the enormous children of human parents, like Tom Hickathrift. Closely related to these monsters are those witches and wizards which are not of mere human origin, for though the Scottish witches were supposed to have close intercourse with the fairies they could not claim anything but mortal blood.

These are only rough divisions for the sake of convenience, and one fairy will seem to belong now to one class and now to another, for we are dealing with the traditions of mixed races, and with oral traditions, coloured differently by each teller. It is no wonder if these fairies seem confused and shifting when some are said to be forgotten gods, some fallen angels, some ghosts, and some almost extinct races.

TYPES OF FAIRIES

PART ONE

THE FAIRY PEOPLE

A. HEROIC FAIRIES

B. TROOPING FAIRIES

C. HOMELY FAIRIES

THE FAIRY PEOPLE

A. HEROIC FAIRIES

THE Heroic Fairies are nearly connected with the small Trooping Fairies, indeed some of the small fairies, like the Cornish Little People and the Irish Gentry are dwindled versions of the Heroic Fairies. The Dana o'Shee, who lived in Tir-nan-Og, the Land of the Ever-Young, are the most obvious example of the Heroic Fairies. The Dana were supposed to be the Danaan Race, who inhabited Ireland before the invasion of the Fenians. They were skilled in metal work and music, far beyond the Fenians who conquered them. After the conquest of Ireland the Danaans retreated to caves and hollows. Their superior skill gave them a magical reputation, and gradually all the Underworld was given over to them. In some stories one day in the Land of the Ever-Young is equal to a minute of human time. But in most stories time in fairyland passes very rapidly, and a man may have been away seven years who only imagines himself to have been away seven minutes. Stories of this different pulse of fairy time come to us from all over the kingdom and from most countries where there are any fairies at all. There is also a fairy or angelic bird, whose singing so enraptures the listener that a hundred years passes as he listens. The question arises of what happens to him while he listens, for he is invisible to humanity while he stands there and un-affected by anything that is happening in the place from which he yet seems never to have moved.

The fairies of the Lowlands of Scotland, or the People of Peace, are of the same type as the Dana O'Shee. The Fairy Queen who took True Thomas away with her was as large as a mortal woman, and the Fairy Court who held Tamlane prisoner was obviously the same. In the Highlands also the same court meets, though it does not ride in such state. Thomas the Rhymer is commonly the go-between who engages human pipers for the fairies' revels. He seems to be Chamberlain to the Fairy Queen.

The dates when fairyland touches the human world most closely are Hallowe'en and Midsummer Eve, when mortals carried away by fairies can be most easily freed. Hallowe'en is a festival also sacred to the dead, and there seems often to be a confusion between the dead and the fairies who live in the barrows and tumuli and use the flint arrow heads which were made by prehistoric men. In Ireland the ghosts and fairies are said to dance together on Hallowe'en.

Very near to these Heroic Fairies are the sleeping heroes who make a yearly ride round their mounds on Midsummer Eve. So King Arthur sleeps in Cadbury Hill and many another old Pictish fort, and rides yearly round it with all his court on Midsummer Eve as the Fairy Court rode when Janet rescued Tamlane from its clutches. And so Earl Fitzgerald rides round the Rath of Mullaghmast.

The belief that the fairies were fallen angels not bad enough for hell is mixed with the idea of the lost Heroic Races, for we see in Tamlane that every seven years the fairies must pay a tribute to hell. These Heroic Fairies have their darker side. No less than the smaller ones they are great kidnappers and sometimes very sinister ones, like the Elf King who carried Burd Helen off to the Dark Tower from which her brother Roland rescued her.

Most of the Heroic Fairies seem to have the power of enlarging and shrinking, as a great many, but not all, fairies have. A good many descriptions of the Fairy Rides are of little people, about the size of children of three years old, riding little shaggy white ponies the size of Newfoundland dogs. Keightley[1] quotes a picturesque description given by an old woman of Nithsdale of the Lowland Fairy Ride.

'In the night afore Roodmass I had trysted with a neebor lass a Scots mile frae hame to talk anent buying braws i' the fair. We had nae sutten lang aneath the

[1] *Fairy Mythology*, p. 355.

21

haw-buss till we heard the loud laugh of fowk riding, wi' the jingling o' bridles, and the clanking o' hoofs. We banged up, thinking they wad ride owre us. We kent nae but it was drunken fowk ridin' to the fair i' the forenight. We glowdired roun' and roun', and sune saw it was the *Fairie-fowks Rade*. We cowred down till they passed by. A beam o' light was dancing owre them mair bonnie than moonshine; they were a' wee, wee fowk wi' green scarfs on, but ane that rode foremost, and that ane was a good deal larger than the lave, wi' bonnie lang hair, bun' about wi' a strap whilk glinted like stars. They rade on braw wee white naigs, wi' unco long swooping tails, an' manes hung wi' whustles that the win' played on. This an' their tongue when they sang was like the soun' o' a far awa' psalm. Marion an' me was in a brade lea fiel' where they came by us; a high hedge o' haw-trees keepit them frae gaun through Johnnie Corrie's corn, but they lap a' owre it like sparrows, and gallopt into a green know beyont it. We gaed i' the morning to look at the treddit corn; but the fient a hoof mark was there, nor a blade broken.'

By the time the fairies left Scotland they seem to have grown rather the worse for wear, for Hugh Miller[1] describes how they were seen on a Sunday morning by a small boy and girl, the only two people who had not gone to church that day.

'The horses were shaggy, diminutive things, speckled dun and gray, the riders stunted, misgrown, ugly creatures, attired in antique jerkins of plaid, long grey clokes and little red caps, from under which their wild

[1] *Old Red Sandstone*, p. 241. Everyman Library.

uncombed locks shot out over their cheeks and fore-heads.'

The boy and his sister watched until all but the last had gone, when the boy said to him: 'What are ye, little mannie, and whaur are ye going?'

'Not of the Race of Adam,' said the little man. 'The People of Peace shall never more be seen in Scotland.'

One of the chief authorities on the Knoll Fairies of Scotland is Robert Kirke, a seventeenth-century Perthshire minister, whose *Secret Commonwealth* gives a very exact picture of fairy beliefs in Scotland. Kirke was credited with strange dealings with the fairies, and when at last he died it was supposed that only a stock had been buried in his grave, and that he himself had been entrapped into a fairy circle.

According to his description: 'These *Siths* or FAIRIES they call *Sleagh Maith*, or the Good People, it would seem, to prevent the Dint of their ill Attempts, (for the Irish use to bless all they fear Harme of;) and are said to be of a midle Nature betwixt Man and Angel, as were Daemons thought to be of old; of intelligent studious Spirits, and light changable Bodies (lyke those called Astral), somewhat of the Nature of a condensed Cloud, and best seen in Twilight. Thes Bodies be so plyable through the Subtilty of the Spirits that agitate them, that they can make them appear or disappear att Pleasure. Some have Bodies or Vehicles so spungious, thin, and desecat, that they are fed by only sucking into some fine spirituous Liquors, that peirce lyke pure Air and Oyl, others feid more gross on the Foyson or substance of Corns and

Liquors, or Corne it selfe that grows on the Surface of the Earth, which these Fairies steall away, partly invisible, partly preying on the Grain, as do Crowes and Mice.'

Kirke later explains how the fairies stole the essential goodness out of corn and milk to nourish themselves in the same way as the witches were supposed to do. The story of the Tacksman's ox illustrates this belief. A common belief mentioned by Kirke is that fairies can only be seen between one blink of an eye and another. To see them longer the eyes must be fixed, and therefore it is considered unlucky to fix the eyes in what is generally called 'a brown study'.

In England the life-sized fairies led a life more like that of the country people near whom they lived, and the Fairy Market could often be seen in the distance. Like one kind of apparition these fairies were perceptible to only one sense at a time. They could be seen from a distance, a crowd of brightly-dressed people chaffering on a green hillside, but when the spectator approached he could see nothing, only felt himself pressed, squeezed and jostled by an invisible crowd.[1]

Some of the Welsh Tylwyth Teg, or Fair Family, are of the same type as the Dana o'Shee. They are of more than mortal size, with fair, flowing hair, and only show themselves to fair-haired mortals. They ride about hunting and revelling, and dance in rings. Some of them live in mounds, but most under water. They wear sometimes white, and sometimes gay colours and rayed coats. The name Tylwyth Teg is used for all

[1] Bovet, *Pandaemonium*, 1684.

types of fairy in Wales, like the Good People in Scotland, and it is sometimes difficult to know which type is spoken of. There are some traces of a complete race of female fairies, very beautiful, who often marry mortals. But it is difficult to be sure of this, as, in one story, the fairy's father appears to give her away. It may only be that the female fairies like to go about in bevies. The Fairy Marriage, with the prohibition, as in 'Wild Edric', is common in Wales. Very often it is that the Fairy Wife may not be struck, or touched with iron.

STORIES

Earl Fitzgerald in the Enchanted Hill[1]

THE Earl Fitzgerald was a great champion against the English, and as great a master of Magic as of War. He and his lady lived together in his Castle of Mullaghmast; but, though his lady had heard of his magical skill, she had seen nothing of it, and she was always begging him to give her some proof of what he could do.

At last he said: 'I can change myself into any shape you like, but if you scream or show any fear at all while I am in my magic shape you will never see me again.'

But his lady was sure she was as brave as any woman living, and she begged him to make the attempt. Earl Fitzgerald muttered a strange word into his beard, and in a moment he was gone and a bright goldfinch flashed round the room.

His lady was startled at the moment, but her nerves were firm, and she soon watched the bird in delight. At last it flew out into the garden — to fetch her a flower she thought — but in a moment it was back with a great hungry falcon close behind it. The falcon was so close that the lady screamed out in terror, so

---

[1] Kennedy, *Legendary Fiction of the Irish Celts.*

that it swerved aside and dashed itself against the wall behind her and fell dead. The lady breathed again in relief; but when she looked for her goldfinch it was nowhere to be found, and she remembered her fatal scream and Earl Fitzgerald's warning.

Since that day the Earl Fitzgerald and his followers have slept an enchanted sleep inside the Rath of Mullaghmast. Only once a year on Midsummer Eve they ride round the Currough of Kildare on milk white horses shod in silver. These silver shoes were half an inch thick when first he was seen, and last time they were as thin as a silver sixpence. When they are as thin as a cat's ear a miller's son with six fingers on each hand will make his way into the cave and blow the horn that hangs there, and at the blast the warriors will wake and sweep the English out of Ireland. Every seven years a door is open into the Rath, and once, more than a hundred years ago, a drunken horse-dealer made his way in. There he saw a great chamber, where the Earl Fitzgerald sat sleeping at the head of a long table, and on each side of it sat his armed warriors, with their heads bowed on the table and each man's steed behind him in its stall. The great armed figures, alive and still, and the silence of the place frightened the man so much that the bridle fell from his hand and clanged hollowly on the floor. At the sound the sleeper next him raised his head and muttered: 'Is the time yet come?'

Nothing terrified the man so much as the thought of that crowd stirring to life again, so he said hastily: 'The time is not yet, but it will be soon.' Then, as the warrior settled himself to sleep again he scrambled from the cave, and left the bridle to be found by the miller's son or any other mortal who might come that way.

PARALLEL STORIES: 'Arthur in Cadbury Hill'; 'True Thomas under Dunmore Hill'.

True Thomas[1]

THOMAS LEARMONT of Ercildoune was sitting on Huntly Bank to listen to the birds' song when he saw a lady riding towards him of more than mortal beauty. She was dressed in green and her horse's mane was hung with tinkling bells. She was so beautiful that he took her to be the Queen of Heaven, but she told him frankly that she was no more than the Queen of Elfland, and that one kiss of his lips on hers would put him in her power. In spite of that he kissed her gladly, and became her bondman for seven years. He mounted behind her, and they rode like the wind to a desert place, where they rested and she showed him three wonders, the Path of Righteousness, narrow and thorny and unfrequented, and the broad, pleasant, well-trodden road to hell, and the pretty, hidden, twisting path which led to fairyland and which they followed. But before they reached fairyland darkness fell, and their horse waded through a roaring torrent of blood, for all the blood shed on earth rises again in the springs of fairyland. When morning came again they were in a pleasant orchard country, where the Queen of Elfland plucked an apple of truth from a tree and gave it to Thomas, with the gift of prophecy. And from that hour on Thomas could speak nothing but the truth, and in fairyland and the mortal world alike he went by the name of True Thomas.

So for seven years True Thomas lived on in fairyland

[1] (Scottish.) Scott, *Ministrelsy of the Scottish Border.*

in great joy, and the Fairy Queen loved him more than any other knight; but at the end of the seven years she grew uneasy for him. For every seven years the fairies are forced to pay a tribute to hell, and the Queen feared that True Thomas would be chosen, for the fairies must pay of their best. So she took him back to the Eildon Tree by Bogle Burn and left him there. But he knew that he was her bondsman still, and must return when she sent for him.

So True Thomas returned to mortal men, and his fairy gifts, song and prophecy, brought him great honour, so that there was no man more sought after in the kingdom. And he lived till he was an old man with a white beard, and his children were many about him. Then one night when there was feasting in Ercildoune and when the Douglas and many other famous knights were gathered to hear his harping, there came news that a white hind and a white doe were passing sedately and unafraid through the town. True Thomas started up and slung his harp behind him.

'They are come for me,' he said. 'And this is the hour that was foretold.' As he spoke they appeared in the doorway and came up to him. When they touched him he followed them, and no man had power to follow or stop them. True Thomas went from amongst his mortal kin in the year thirteen hundred or a little earlier; but the man who visits fairyland may see him yet, the great deviser of the fairies' sports and the chief Harper amongst them all.

PARALLEL STORIES: There are none very similar in

incident to 'True Thomas', though there are many stories of visits to fairyland. 'The Return of Oisin', which follows, has some resemblance, but enough points of difference to make it worth telling.

THE RETURN OF OISIN[1]

THERE are many stories of Fionn of the Fianna Finn and his friendships, loves and conflicts with the people of O'Shee, both good and bad, but this is the story of the last of the Fianna Finn, Fionn's son Oisin the poet, the gentlest and most beautiful of the Fianna Finn.

One day the whole Fianna were hunting, as they used to do in times of peace, along the banks of Loch Leinn, when they saw a rider coming towards them on a milk white horse. When she drew near they saw that it was a maiden so beautiful that even Fionn had never seen and could hardly imagine anyone to rival her. The great champions drew around her, and Fionn begged to know if they might serve her in any way.

'My name is Niam of the Golden Hair,' she said. 'My father is King of Tir-nan-Og, the Land of the Ever-Young; and I have come to see your son Oisin, of whom I have heard even in Tir-nan-Og.'

'This is a good day to me when I see you,' said Oisin. 'And a good day when I hear you say this. But it will be an ill day for me when you leave me, for I am ready to follow beyond the rim of the world for one glance of your eye.'

'If that be so,' said Niam, 'mount behind me, and I will carry you to the Land of the Ever-Young, which flows with milk and wine, where we can live together in joy for more years than you can reckon.'

At these words Fionn stretched out his hands to his

[1] (Irish.) From the Poem by Michael Comyn.

son, and all the Fianna set up a bitter cry at the thought of losing their best beloved. But Oisin's heart was gone from him with love for Niam of the Golden Hair, and he mounted behind her, and she shook her tinkling bridle, and the horse sped away.

They rode until they came to the Western Sea, where the horse shook itself and rose up into the air, and so they sped on. At night they rested on an island where one of the Princesses of the O'Shee was imprisoned by a loathesome Fomorian, whom Oisin fought and killed. Next day they pressed on until they reached the Island of Tir-nan-Og, where Niam's father and mother received them gladly and they were married. In feasting and dancing and song, in hunting and the delights of love they spent three happy years. Then Oisin's heart began to reproach him that he had so long forgotten his father and his old companions, and he begged Niam to let him go back to see them again.

'You do not know,' she said, 'how quickly time passes in that world. It will be too late to go back now.'

'All the more reason to go back quickly,' said Oisin, and he was so unhappy at the thought that his father might be growing old without him that at last she lent him the milk white horse to return.

'But be careful,' she said, 'that all the time you are there you never dismount from his back, nor once touch the ground with your foot.'

Oisin promised, and rode back to the shores of Ireland. The whole land looked small and shrivelled to his eyes. The hills were rounder and smaller, the streams were shrunken, the forests were thinner. He rode to Loch Leinn, and it seemed to him that there must have been a great drought there that summer, for it was by a third smaller than it had been when he hunted there last. In the distance he saw some men, and he rode over to them; but when he got near he saw that they were small and stunted, on poor little horses, and they for their part looked with fear at the great golden warrior, towering above them on his milk white horse. At the sight of them fear and strangeness came upon Oisin, and he rode as fast as he could to the Hill of Allen in Kildare, where his father's castle stood. There were only rough mounds and half-covered stones left of the castle, and as he rode round it he heard the jangling of strange bells in the distance; for three hundred years had passed since he left the shores of Ireland, the Fianna had gone, and Christianity had crept into the land.

Oisin turned his horse's head towards the sea, for there was no one left to welcome him, and he longed for Tir-nan-Og. But as he went he passed by Glen Ashmole, and saw a crowd of the little men whom he had seen before struggling to lift a great stone which lay at the head of the Glen. It would have been heavy, even for one of the Fianna, and these smaller men were in danger of being crushed by it. Oisin admired the courage with which they struggled, and, bending from his horse, he lifted the stone for them and set it on end. But the weight of the great stone twisted round the girth on his horse's belly, and Oisin fell his length on the ground.

As soon as he left the saddle the white horse started

34

and plunged, and galloped like the wind towards the West. And the people round the stone fell back, for where a great golden youth had fallen to the ground an old shrivelled man arose from it, bent under the weight of three hundred years.

So Oisin, the last of the Fianna, was left alone in Ireland; and, because he was the gentlest of them, he gladly became a Christian, and lived on, telling wonderful tales of old days with the Fianna Finn, and died in the odour of sanctity at last. But some say he never rested in churchyard mould, but went back to the Land of Tir-nan-Og and to the embraces of Niam of the Golden Hair.

PARALLEL STORIES: There are many parallels to this all over the world. One of the closest is the Japanese story of 'The Fisherman and the Mermaid'. The Highland story of 'The Two Fiddlers' has the same miraculous passage of time.

THE TACKSMAN AND THE OX[1]

IT is well known that the fairies can steal the substance from our food and cattle and yet leave them apparently unimpaired, unless spells are used to prevent it. The Tacksman of Auchriachan near Glenlivet knew this, and was always most careful to use the spells taught him by his grandmother so as to preserve his food for his own use. One evening, however, his goats had strayed, and as he followed them up the sides of Glenlivet a thick mist came down, and he began to fear that he would never see the morning. He sat down to wait until the mist had cleared; but presently in the distance he saw a light, and when he came up to it he saw that it came from a curious dwelling, almost as if a part of the hill had been raised upon pillars. He knocked at the open doorway, and a woman came to the door whose face he knew well. He had been at her funeral a few months before.

'What in the name of wonder are you doing here, Auchriachan?' she said. 'Get you home at once, for my companions are unchancey people for you to meet if they come back before you are gone.'

'I cannot go, Janet woman,' he said. 'The mist is thick around me, and I cannot stir a foot without falling down a cliff. You must make some hiding place for me and take me in.'

Janet was an old friend, so she hid him in a corner of the room and piled peats round him. In a little time the fairies came in, led by an old man, with a long

[1] (Highland.) Keightley, *Fairy Mythology*, p. 390.

white beard and a silver chain whom the rest called True Thomas, so that Auchriachan knew him to be no other than Thomas the Rhymer, who had disappeared into fairyland two hundred years before.

The fairies came in very hungry, and began to ask each other how they should dine.

'The Tacksman of Auchriachan has a fine fat ox,' said True Thomas. 'The old miser guards it carefully enough with his spells as a rule; but our friends the goats have led him away tonight, and his son has forgotten the spell; let us fetch it and roast it.'

The others shouted with joy, and in a minute some of them came back with the body of Auchriachan's poor ox, which was roasted under his eye.

'But what shall we do for bread?' said one fairy, as the ox was cooking.

'I noticed that Auchriachan's wife had forgotten to make a cross on her bannocks,' said one who had brought the ox. 'We can take those.'

Poor Auchriachan could hardly contain himself at this second theft; but for the love of life he had to lie quiet; and as the fairies were about it Janet hurried him out, for the mist had blown aside. Auchriachan hurried home to see how much damage had been done. There he found his ox and his wife's bannocks looking as well as ever; but the bannocks had no cross on them, and his son confessed that he had forgotten to say any words over the ox that night.

So Auchriachan felled the ox, and threw it and the bread out on the brae side, where neither cat nor dog came near them, for indeed all the good had been taken out of them to the fairy knowe.

The Green Children[1]

ANOTHER wonderful thing happened in Suffolk, at
St. Mary's of the Wolf-pits. A boy and his sister were
found by the inhabitants of that place near the mouth
of a pit which is there, who had the form of all their
limbs like to those of other men, but they differed in
the colour of their skin from all the people of our
habitable world; for the whole surface of their skin was
tinged of a green colour. No one could understand
their speech. When they were brought as curiosities
to the house of a certain knight, Sir Richard de Calne,
at Wikes, they wept bitterly. Bread and other victuals
were set before them, but they would touch none of
them, though they were tormented by great hunger, as
the girl afterwards acknowledged. At length, when
some beans just cut, with their stalks, were brought
into the house, they made signs, with great avidity,
that they should be given to them. When they were
brought, they opened the stalks instead of the pods,
thinking the beans were in the hollow of them; but not
finding them there, they began to weep anew. When
those that were present saw this, they opened the pods
and showed them the naked beans. They fed on these
with great delight, and for a long time tasted no other
food. The boy, however, was always languid and
depressed, and he died within a short time. The girl
enjoyed continual good health; and becoming accus-
tomed to various kinds of food, lost completely that

[1] (English.) 'William of Newbridge', quoted by Keightley, p. 281.

green colour, and gradually recovered the sanguine habit of her entire body. She was afterwards regenerated by the laver of holy baptism, and lived for many years in the service of that knight (as I have frequently heard from him and his family), and was rather loose and wanton in her conduct.

Being frequently asked about the people of her country, she asserted that the inhabitants, and all they had in that country, were of a green colour; and that they saw no sun, but enjoyed a degree of light like what is after sunset. Being asked how she came into this country with the aforesaid boy, she replied, that as they were following their flocks, they came to a certain cavern, on entering which they heard a delightful sound of bells; ravished by whose sweetness, they went on for a long time wandering through the cavern, until they came to its mouth. When they came out of it, they were struck senseless by the excessive light of the sun, and the unusual temperature of the air; and they thus lay for a long time. Being terrified by the noise of those who came on them, they wished to fly, but they could not find the entrance of the cavern before they were caught.

PARALLEL STORIES: In the later stories we have some anecdotes of fairies caught by mortals, but none quite like this curious fragment of medieval folk gossip.

WILD EDRIC[1]

IN the days of William the Norman a famous champion called Wild Edric lived near the Forest of Clun. One day as he was hunting in the forest he lost his way, and, with his little page, wandered to and fro, till it was dark. At length he saw a light in the forest, and in the very wildest part found a fair and large house. The light streamed from it into the dark forest, and, looking in from outside, he saw a great company of women dancing. They were clothed in fine linen, taller and more beautiful all of them than mortal women; but one seemed to him to outshine all the rest,

and as he looked on her his mind was inflamed with love. He was sure that he was looking on a company of elf-maidens, but there was no room in his mind for fear, and he went boldly round the place until he found the door. He went in, followed by his page, and through the throng of the dancers until he reached

[1] Miss Burne, *Shropshire Folk Lore*.

40

the elf-maiden on whom his love was laid. He seized hold of her. All her sisters gathered round to protect her; but with the help of his page he carried her off, and they made their way out into the night again, scratched and bleeding, but with the elf-maiden in Edric's arms.

Somehow they found their way home; but the elf-maiden would neither look at Edric nor speak to him for four long days, do what he could to please her. At the end of four days she suddenly looked up and smiled.

'Good luck be with you, my dear,' she said. 'You have me now, and I will be your wife, and we have a good hope of happiness if you will remember one thing. Never reproach me with my kin nor question my absences, for if you do I shall be snatched away, and you will pine without me.'

Edric promised to be careful, and they were married in great happiness, and so they lived for many years. The news of the strange bride went even as far as London, and the King summoned Edric to bring his wife to town. The whole court were eager to hear the tale, and the elf-wife's beauty was such that all believed it, and the two went with honour back to Shropshire. There was only one thing that troubled Wild Edric, and that was that his wife was sometimes mysteriously away for long hours. But he remembered her warning and asked nothing. One day, however, he returned from hunting, eager to tell his wife his day's sport. He called and looked, but she was nowhere to be found. At last, after many hours, she came quietly downstairs to him.

'You've been long enough away this time,' he said. 'I suppose it was your sisters kept you.'

They were the last words he said to her, and before he had finished he was speaking to air. He searched for her like a man distracted, and rode through and through the Forest of Clun, looking for the house where her sisters had danced. But he found no trace of it, and in a few months he pined away and died.

PARALLEL STORIES: 'The Spirit of the Van', Keightley; 'The Shepherd of Drws Coed', Sikes.

TAMLANE[1]

THE wood of Carterhaugh was haunted ground. It was said that Tamlane, an elfin knight, guarded it, and that the maiden whom he caught there must pay tribute in golden ring or green mantle or maidenhood. But Janet counted Carterhaugh her own, for her father had given it her, and she braided her hair and kilted her skirt and ran into the wood to pick wild roses. There was a horse standing saddled and bridled by the spring in the wood, but no rider was to be seen, and she began to pick her roses without fear. She had hardly broken one when a little man in green started up and caught her by the hand. Janet gave him back word for word fearlesssly, but for all that she paid her tribute, and went back to her father's hall without her maidenhood and with only half her heart.

Time went by and Janet grew troubled about her lover, whom she could have loved more than any man if he had been a human knight and not an elf. So at last she went back to Carterhaugh and plucked the briers again to call Tamlane to her side.

He started up angrily; but when he heard that Janet wished to free him from fairyland his heart softened with hope. He was no fairy by birth, but the son of a neighbour, who had been stolen at nine years old. Fairyland was full of pleasures, he had powers beyond human powers, he could make himself small or large,

[1] (Scottish.) A Border Ballad. Scott, *Minstrelsy of the Scottish Border*. Blackwood, 1902. Vol. II, p. 388.

he could make horses out of rushes; all delights of food and drink and pleasure were theirs, and he was a favourite with the Queen; but the time was coming when the tribute to hell must be paid, and he began to be afraid that he would be chosen. So he told Janet how she must rescue him.

On Hallowe'en the Fairy Court would be riding, and Janet must be standing for safety by the Miles Cross, with a stoup of water beside her and a stoup of milk. She must let the first company pass her and then the second, and Tamlane would be in the third. The black steed and the brown would pass her, and Tamlane would be riding on the white, with one hand gloved and one hand bare. She must run and pull him off his horse and hold him, whatever shapes they turned him into, and at the last she must throw her mantle over him and he would be saved.

So Janet went to the Miles Cross on the cold last night of October, and crouched beside it to watch the Seeley Court ride by. Presently she heard the ringing of fairy bells, and one company after another came jingling merrily past her. She peered with all her might at the third, and saw Tamlane on his white horse, and ran and pulled him down. There was a shriek from all around her, and she felt him for a moment under her hands, then he dwindled down, and she felt a slimy newt struggling in her tightened grasp; but she held it firm and stepped back to Miles Cross as the fairies pressed about her. As she moved, she felt the shape alter, and there was an adder struggling to turn back and sink its fangs into her hand; but she held it firmly for all that. Then the thing

44

began to glow, and she saw a faggot in her hands; but she held firmly to it. Then she felt a fiery heat, and it was turning into a red-hot iron gad; but she did not let go, only dipped it and her hands into the milk and then into the water till it was quenched, and turned to a toad and then an eel, which she lifted out of the water, and as she lifted it it became a fluttering dove, and at last a great, strong swan, beating its white wings until she could hardly hold it. But this noblest transformation was his last, and in a moment he lay in her arms, a spent, naked man, and she threw her mantle over him and made him hers. As she did so the fairies around set up a harsh wail and the Fairy Queen cried out in a bitter voice that had she known of Tamlane's treachery Janet should never have gotten a whole knight as her love; his eyes should have been of wood and his heart of stone, or he should have gone before his time to pay their debt to hell. So she vanished railing away, and Tamlane went home with Janet and married her.

PARALLEL STORIES: Two more stories follow about rescue from fairyland, and there are several more in the section on the Trooping Fairies.

CHILDE ROLAND [1]

CHILDE ROLAND was one of the stories that Shakespeare knew, for the Fool in *King Lear* quotes it.

Childe Roland lived with his two brothers and his mother and his sister, Burd Helen, for his father was dead. One day Childe Roland and his brothers were playing at football together, and Childe Roland gave the ball such a kick that it flew right over the church to the other side. Burd Helen, like the good sister she was, ran to fetch it, but she ran widdershins, that is — against the sun. She did not come back, so they went to look for her, and they found her nowhere about the church, nor anywhere at home. They called and hunted, but she was nowhere to be seen. A week passed and a month, and when a year had gone the eldest brother decided to go out into the world to look for her. So he girded on his good sword and, by his mother's advice, went to seek counsel of the Wizard Merlin, who would help him if anyone could.

Merlin hardly needed to hear his story before he gave the remedy.

'Burd Helen,' he said, 'went widdershins the church, so that her shadow fell behind her. The King of Elfland must have caught her by the shadow and carried her away. If you wish to reach Elfland go by this way and by that, the way is not hard to find. But take your good sword by your side, and remember when you reach Elfland you must cut the head off any

[1] (English.) Jacobs, *English Fairy Tales*, p. 115.

creature that will speak to you, and if you wish to win free from there you must neither bite a bit nor drink a drop.'

This sounded plain enough, and the eldest son went off with a good courage. But he never returned. So after a year of waiting the second went, and heard the same counsel and set out the same way. And he too never returned. So the widowed Queen was left with Childe Roland for her only comfort, and after a time he too begged to go. His mother at first could hardly bear to part with him, but he was so wretched at the thought that his brothers might be waiting for his help that at length she gave him his father's great sword and let him go. He went to Merlin, as his brothers had done, and pondered deeply what he had been told.

It was some way to Elfland, but the path was clear enough; and one evening he felt a different taste in the air and saw the grass a brighter green, and knew himself in Elfland. A small, wizened man was watching a herd of small shaggy ponies with fiery eyes, and as Roland drew near he lifted his eyes, and they too shone like a cat's eyes in the moonlight. Then Roland said:

'This must be the King of Elfland's horseherd. Tell me quickly where the Dark Tower of Elfland stands.'

47

But the horseherd said: 'Go on till you come to the King of Elfland's Cowherd. He will know.'

Roland murmured a word of thanks, and he was passing on when he saw a flash of joy in the fiery eyes, and he remembered what Merlin had said. So he cried: 'Out, sword!' and with one blow he swept the horseherd's head from his body. The horseherd never stayed nor faltered in his stride for that, but picked up his head, and went on with his work with it tucked under his arm; and Childe Roland went on his way.

The next living things he saw were a herd of dwarfish, shaggy cattle and an old man in green watching them, who raised his head and looked at Roland as bleakly as the east wind on a cold day.

Then Childe Roland said: 'This must be the King of Elfland's cowherd. Tell me quickly where the Dark Tower of Elfland stands.'

The cowherd answered singingly: 'I know not, I know not; maybe the henwife knows.'

This time Childe Roland did not hesitate. He cried again: 'Out, sword!' and swept the cowherd's head off his shoulders, and the cowherd picked it up and melted like mist. And Childe Roland had hardly gone a few paces when he saw an old woman with a rosy face feeding tiny cocks and hens. As he came up she turned her head and fixed him with a pair of pale, dry, motionless eyes. And Roland said: 'Oh stony-eyed wife, tell me quickly where the Dark Tower of Elfland stands.'

'There,' said the henwife, and Roland saw the great dark tumulus which hid the King of Elfland's Palace.

He pressed on so eagerly that he would have forgotten the henwife if he had not heard a tiny chuckle behind him as he passed her. Then he cried: 'Out, sword, out!' and he swept her head from its body and pressed on to the Dark Tower. He went three times round it widdershins and stamped three times on the ground, and he cried: 'Open hill, open door!' and a door in the dark hillside opened wide.

Inside there was a beam of bright light, and Burd Helen stood in it, smiling and crying out: 'Welcome, dear brother!'

But Childe Roland with his good sword still in his hand swept it round and cut her beautiful head clean from her shoulders, and the whole hillside shook and the beautiful shape vanished, and the real Burd Helen ran pale and trembling to his arms. They kissed each other and wept, and Childe Roland remembering that he needed strength to fight the Elf King, said: 'Get me something to eat and drink, Burd Helen, for I am wearied, and I have yet to fight the King of Elfland.'

Burd Helen was still tongue-tied, and she looked sadly at him and fetched him food, and wine in a curiously chased goblet. Childe Roland raised the goblet to his lips, but before he drank he smiled to his sister as befitted his courtly training, and the look on her face reminded him of what Merlin had said.

'Not a bit must I bite! Not a drop must I drink!' he cried, and hurled the cup to the ground. And as it clanged the Dark Tower resounded with the Elf King's footsteps, who cried in a terrible voice:

'Fee! Fi! Fo! Fum!
I smell the blood of a Christian Man.
Be he dead, be he living, with this brand
I'll dash his brains from his brain pan!'

Then Childe Roland cried: 'Out, sword, out! Strike, sword, now, or never strike again!' and he rushed at the Elf King, and they foined and smote and parried up and down the Great Hall of the Dark Tower. At length Childe Roland beat the grim Elf King to the ground; and with his foot on his throat and his sword at his heart he promised him death unless he would bring his two brothers back to life and set Burd Helen free. And scowling up at him the Elf King said: 'They shall be free.'

Then he went to a cupboard in the wall and brought out a crystal jar of red clear oil, and he anointed the hands and nostrils of the two brothers, who lay there stiff and frozen, and their pale lips and their heavy eyelids, so that they started up alive and laughing with joy, and ran to Burd Helen's side. And all four ran through the gates of the Dark Tower and out of Elfland. So they went home to their mother with great rejoicing, and as long as she lived Burd Helen never went widdershins a church again.

The Fairies and the Smith[1]

There was once a smith on Islay who had an only son, a boy of fourteen, merry and handsome and beloved. But one day when the smith came in from the forge he found the boy lying on his bed in the kitchen, silent and pale, a changed creature. He would eat and drink, but he neither spoke nor smiled, and at length in despair his father went for counsel to a second-sighted man who lived near.

'It has the look to me,' said the Wise Man, 'as if your son had been carried off by the People of Peace. But you must make sure.' And he told him what to do.

So the smith went home and got together all the empty eggshells he could find. And in the morning, when he had redded up the house, he began to draw his water, but instead of taking the pails he went out with a pair of eggshells and brought them and balanced them by the fire. So he brought them in two by two till he had twenty ranged together, and the boy sat up in the bed to watch. At length he could contain himself no longer, but cried out: 'Ho! Ho! I have lived eight hundred years, but I never saw water drawn in eggshells before!'

At that the smith piled fuel on the fire with so black a look that the thing on the bed misdoubted him.

'What are you doing that for?' it said.

'You will soon see,' said the smith, and he lifted the creature in his arms and threw it on the fire. It never

[1] (Highland.) Campbell, *Tales of the Western Highlands.*

touched the flames, but with a great scatter and whiffling flew up the chimney and away. The smith turned to embrace his own dear child, but nothing was there, and though he hunted all around, hoping to find him somewhere, he never came. So the smith went again to the Wise Man.

'They hold your child very jealously,' he said. 'He has been too long in their power, or he is too old to be regained so easily. If you would have him again you must seek him in the Green Rath when the moon is full.'

It is a brave man who ventures into the Fairy Hills, but the smith was ready to do anything for the love of his son, so he learned carefully what he must do, and waited till the moon was full. He took with him a dirk and a bible and a live cock hidden under his plaid; for the three things the People of Peace hate are cold iron and the Word of God and the sound of cockcrow. As he came near to the Rath he heard the faint sound of faraway pipes, and saw the mound raised up upon pillars with the light flooding from it. He stuck his dirk into the grass by the doorway and went boldly in. The place was full of light and dancing, but beyond them the smith saw his son toiling at a great forge, with many more like him. As he came in the music faltered, and the dancers came twittering around him with a cry like bats. But though their arms were stretched out against him they could not touch him because of the Bible which he carried.

'Give me my son,' said the smith, 'and I will go.'

'Hold him here! Shut down the hill!' said some, and one pillar after another sank into the earth; but

52

the doorway by which the smith had entered did not close, for the cold iron held it open.

Then the Little People came buzzing round the smith, screaming one after another and all together:

'We have your son! We will keep him! He is ours! We will keep him!'

But there was one more in the company than they knew of. The cock had dozed till now under the cover of the plaid, but the clamour roused him. He struggled free from the smith's arms, flew up to his shoulder, and crowed loud and long. At the hated sound the lights popped out in the Fairy Hill, and the People of Peace fled shrieking to the darkest corners. The smith strode over to his son and caught him in the pale glow of the furnace. Then the People of Peace came round them again and thrust them out of the hill. The dirk was shot out after them, the hillside closed down, and they felt the wholesome night air on them again.

53

But for a year and a day the smith had no joy of his conquest. His boy sat brooding, almost as listless, dunt and idle as the changeling had been; until one day his father was working at a delicately wrought sword which was beyond his skill, and the boy said suddenly:

'That is not the way.'

He shaped a better sword than his father had ever seen, and from that day he was himself again. And since he never forgot his fairy skill he became famous through all the countryside.

PARALLEL STORIES: 'The Brewing with Eggshells'; Mrs. Nelson; 'Mr. Kirke's Disappearance'; 'The Young Man in the Shian'. An unusual feature of this story is the blacksmith work which the boy is doing. This rather suggests the ironworking goblins than the iron-hating People of Peace. It is a very complete account of the method of driving out a changeling and freeing a captive from fairyland. The two do not generally occur in one story.

B. TROOPING FAIRIES

THE Trooping Fairies are by far the largest division of the Fairy People, and perhaps the most constant in their general characteristics. It is they who make the fairy rings; they are fond of music and dancing, very sensitive to insults and slights, but ready to reward virtue. They are, as a rule, great lovers of order.

The Muryans, or Small People of Cornwall, are a fair sample of them.[1] These are reputed to be a race who lived in Britain before Christian times, and were too good for hell but not good enough for heaven. So they were allowed to live on on earth, but shrinking year by year from more than mortal size until at length they turn into ants, and so die. For this reason the Cornish people are very careful to avoid hurting

[1] Hunt, *Popular Romances of the West of England,* pp. 81 and 130.

muryans (as ants are called there) for they have a good will for the Small People. The muryans visit human houses at night, and if water is not left out for them they wash their babies in the milk. They are very benevolent towards human beings, and willingly lend them money, food or clothes; but they are exact about the return of the loans at the specified time. Like nearly all other fairies they covet human children.

The fairies of Devon are much like the Cornish Little People. One old woman,[1] who gave a lively description of them, said that they were only a few inches high, but wore very high-heeled shoes, in which they danced upon her cakes and made pock marks, unless she crossed them. Another old woman[2] who was bed-ridden, was much entertained by the visits of the fairies, who played about all over the room, climbed up her bed and danced on the counterpane. Words failed her to describe the airs and graces of the fairy women, or their sauciness to the fairy men. These little fairies seemed to be dressed in the height of modern fashion, and to be like tiny people in their behaviour. Kirke says that the fairies dress commonly in the fashion of the country they inhabit, and describes the Sleagh Maith as wearing tartan. In the Lowlands of Scotland and over a great part of England the fairy colour is green. The Irish fairies most commonly wear little red caps, though there are green fairies in Ireland too. The Tylwyth Teg, some of whom are small like the South Country fairies, though not quite so small, wear dresses of various colours, some green, some rayed

[1] Keightley, p. 304.   [2] Hunt, p. 120.

and some of a white substance which looks rather like paper. Hunt's Cornish Little People are unlike most folk fairies in being dressed in gauze — unless, indeed, that is an embellishment of his own. Other names for these small and generally friendly fairies are the Bendith y Mamau in Glamorganshire, the Ellyllon in all parts of Wales, the Pharisees in Sussex, Warwickshire and Worcestershire, and Trows in the Shetland Isles. Their characteristics are constant. They love dancing and revelry, they must not be talked of or watched. They are generous in their rewards, but withdraw their favour if the rewards are spoken of. They covet human babies. They are sometimes anxious about their own salvation, and consult the clergy or pious men to know if the Bible makes any mention of them. There are as well some rather different types of Trooping Fairies.

The Pisgies or Pixies are more mischievous than the Little People. They are great child stealers, and delight in misleading night travellers, who must turn their coats to avoid being pixy-led. The pretty little Hampshire Thieving Fairies are surely of the same family as the pixies. Sometimes pixies do brownies' work. Of the same nature are those fairies, known in Scotland, Ireland and the south of England, who, riding on grass stalks, or rushes, visit far-off cellars and carouse in them till morning. Perhaps it is those that the Irish see when they take off their hats to a cloud of dust, and wish it 'God speed ye'. It is fairies of pixy nature who ride human horses, sometimes almost to death, hundreds to a horse, whose mane they knot to make fairy stirrups.

The elves are a debatable class. In Anglo-Saxon times the word elf stood for spirit, and all kinds of fairies from witches to the little midnight dancers were called elves. In the early stories the elves were of life size, and often formidable characters like the Elf King in 'Childe Roland'. Later the expression narrowed down to something not unlike the Scandinavian Light Elves, little light-hearted people whose chief business was among flowers. When the fairies became fashionable among the Elizabethan poets, the little fairy boys, the pages of the Fairy Court, were called elves.

> 'Some war with rere-mice for their leathern wings
> To make my small elves coats.'

says Titania. And Milton speaks of the 'pert fairies and the dapper elves' as companions.

The Spriggans are a more sinister kind of fairy. They are Cornish, and are said to be the ghosts of the old giants, whose buried treasures they guard. Though generally tiny they have the power of swelling to immense size. They are dangerous and hideous.

Even worse are the Redcaps, which haunt the ruined Border keeps where wicked things have been done, and who try to dye their red caps redder in the blood of human victims.

The Buccas, or Knockers, are another kind of Cornish Fairy, who haunt the mines and are supposed to be the ghosts of the Jews who once owned them. They are generally friendly to the miners. Other mining fairies are the Coblynau of Wales. These are hideous little fairies with copper-coloured faces, and

dressed in red. They are friendly to the miners, but are not very safe to meet on their holidays, when they dance in the open country. They are obviously the Welsh variant of the goblins, who are not so often met in Britain as in Scandinavia.

These Trooping Fairies range in size from being about the bigness of a three-year-old child to a creature so small that a grain of oats is a heavy load for it. In appearance some are fair-haired, like the Shetland peeries and the Tylwyth Teg of Wales, and some are swarthy and blackhaired. One never hears any mention of their having wings. The closest connection between fairies and wings is in Devon, where the pale moths that come round the candle at night are called pisgies and said to be the souls of unbaptized children, just as the pixies are said to be in other parts of the country. But, with wings or without, these little fairies have no difficulty in travelling through the air, sometimes on grass-stalks, sometimes on dust and sometimes, it seems, by the mere power of their will.

STORIES

BETTY STOGS AND THE LITTLE PEOPLE[1]

THERE was once a drunken slattern of a woman who had a husband pretty nearly as bad as she was herself. How such a couple came to have so fine a baby as they had passed the neighbours' comprehension; but a beautiful child it was, fair and buxom and merry. For all that, Betty Stogs had no pride in it; but the poor little thing went dirty and neglected all day long while its mother gossiped about the place and its father worked or drank.

One evening Betty returned from her visiting and unlocked the door. There was no sound from her baby, and she thought it must have cried itself to sleep. But its coggan was empty. She searched all over the house, but found no sign of it. Then she remembered with horror that the door had been locked. She flew down the hillside to meet her husband and tell him of their loss. The news of it sobered him, and he called in the neighbours to help in the search. They searched all night, but found no trace of the child, and were ready to despair. But when the sun rose the cat rushed into the house with its tail like a bottle brush. It ran to and fro, into the house and out again, miaowing until they followed it.

There, under a bank by the streamside, lay the baby, sleeping on the mossy ground, as sweet and clean as you could wish any baby to be. It was heaped round

[1] Hunt, p. 103.

with flowers, with a bunch of violets in its hand like a child prepared for burial, but it was as well and strong as possible, and more beautiful than it had ever been before.

The neighbours looked at each other and whispered that the Good People must have taken the child to

clean it, and no wonder, when one thought how ill it was usually kept. The child must have been so dirty that one night's cleaning was not enough for the fastidious Little People; so they had left it there to wait till the next night.

Betty snatched up the baby. Her heart had been so pierced by anxiety that night that she was a different woman ever afterwards. The house was clean, and her husband was ready to stay in it. As for the baby, the fairies never came for him again, for from this time on he was kept as the fairies had left him, and the orderly Little People never needed to wash him again.

THE FAIRY FUNERAL[1]

As a rule the fairies are unable to enter a church; the very sound of bells or the sight of a Bible will frighten them away. But the Cornish Little People are so harmless that even a church has no terrors for them.

One night a poor fisherman called Richard, coming home late from St. Ives, heard a faint tolling of the bell of Lelant Church. He went towards it curiously, and saw light streaming from the windows. He scrambled up to one of the windows and looked in. The church was full of tiny people in gauzy clothes with wreaths of flowers on their heads and flowery branches in their hands. They seemed very sad, and six of them carried a bier on which a lovely little figure was lying. The bier all round it was heaped high with flowers, but Richard could see the face, 'as if it were a seraph' for loveliness. There was a tiny hole dug near the altar into which the little body was lowered. Then all the mourners broke their branches crying out: 'Our Queen is dead! Our Queen is dead!'

The grave had yet to be covered, and when the first spadeful of earth fell on her face the ladies broke out with such a shrill wail that Richard cried out too. In an instant the lights were all out, and, with a buzz like a swarm of bees, the fairies flew towards him. Richard slipped down from the window and ran for dear life, with the fairies after him. Indeed, he always counted himself lucky to have escaped with his life. For a swarm of fairies is more dangerous than the wildest swarm of bees that ever took wing.

[1] Hunt, p. 102.

The Thieving Fairies [1]

A HAMPSHIRE farmer was very much puzzled by the state of his barn. The corn would be left every night in orderly piles, but every morning it would be found tossed about in the wildest confusion. At length he determined to hide in his barn and see if he could find out what was happening. All was quiet for a time, but as it drew near midnight the farmer was roused from a short doze by a stir in the barn. The moon was streaming in from the loft above, and struck upon the keyhole; and suddenly the farmer saw crowds of tiny people swarming through it and jumping to the ground. They tossed the corn about and played with it until the place was in the wildest confusion;  but their play was so pretty to watch that the farmer was ready to forgive them a little disarray. Presently, however, they began to carry off the corn, swarming in and out of the keyhole with a grain at a time. They were so many and so rapid that the piles of corn began to show much smaller, and the farmer watched in dismay. But he did not know what the Little People could do to him; so fear kept him silent.

At length, however, one of the Little People said to another in the tiniest voice a human could hear:

[1] Keightley, p. 305.

'I weat, you weat?' At that the farmer forgot his prudence and jumped up.

'The devil sweat ye! Let me get ye!'

At the great roaring he made, the poor Little People dropped their corn and whisked out through the key-hole. Indeed, they had been so frightened that they never came back to the barn again as long as the farmer lived.

PARALLEL STORY: 'Brother Mike', *Suffolk Folk Lore*.

Horse and Hattock [1]

THE Laird of Duffus was out walking in his fields one day when a cloud of dust came whirling past him, and a flight of fairies mounted on grass stalks landed quite near. Presently he heard shrill voices crying: 'Horse and Hattock!' and, being a bold man, he repeated the cry after them, and was immediately swirled away in their midst to the King of France's cellar, where they caroused merrily all night long. Unfortunately, the Laird of Duffus drank too well; and when the cry of 'Horse and Hattock' was raised again he was too drowsy to repeat it. So the Royal Butler found him next morning, still asleep, in the King's cellar, with a cup of curious workmanship in his hand. He was taken before the King, and frankly told him all that had happened. The King pardoned him and dismissed him. He returned home with the fairy cup, which was kept in his family for generations.

PARALLEL STORIES: The Irish story of 'The Carousing Witches'; 'The Pisgies in the Cellar', Hunt.

[1] Scott, *Minstrelsy of the Scottish Border*.

THE MISER AND THE FAIRY FEAST[1]

IT was well known all over St. Just that the Little People held their revels on the Gump when the moon was full. They hardly seemed to mind human observation, and many of their human friends had visited them, and received small but valuable presents. It was the rumour of these presents which allured an old miser living in St. Just to pay the Gump a visit. He set out by the clear light of the Harvest Moon and as he toiled up the Gump he heard music all around him. It was soft but compelling, so that when it was merry he was forced to dance and caper, and when it changed to a sadder note he wept. But where it came from puzzled him, until he had climbed to the top of the Gump, when he was certain that it came from directly under his feet. Suddenly it grew much louder; the hill beneath him opened with a blaze of light and an immense procession of tiny people came out. They seemed to pay no attention to him, though he crouched gaunt and black in the white moonlight; only a company of Spriggans, who were the first to come out, surrounded him.

The Spriggans were the only ugly creatures of the multitude; after them came a great number of fairy children in gauze and gold, who scattered flowers as they went. And the great beauty of the flowers was that they rooted themselves as they touched the earth, so that the hillside was soon a mass of primroses and

[1] Hunt, p. 98.

all sweet, low-growing flowers. Then out came the
little knights in green and gold, and their bevies of
fairy ladies, singing more beautifully than nightingales,
and then the tiny, beautiful King and Queen. They
all moved up to the top of the Gump, and settled
themselves in their thousands at the banquet that
appeared there. It was a sight which no man that saw

it could forget, though he lived to be a hundred.
Every furze bush around the hill glittered with fairy
lights; the whole ground was starred with tiny flowers,
and the air sweet with the scent of them. Each little
figure of the thousands which sat at the feast was
perfect in form and feature. Only the Spriggans who
guarded the outer ring were grotesque and forbidding,
even in their tiny size.

But a man can see only what he is able to see; and
the miser's whole heart was set on the minute golden
plates and cups on which the feast was served; and on

the golden thrones of the King and Queen. He threw himself flat on the ground, and crawled on his belly like a snake round the Gump to the back of the King's throne. All behind him was darkness, all in front of him was light. With his eyes fixed greedily on the riches before him he never noticed that he was surrounded by his guard of Spriggans.

He crawled inch by inch up to the throne, and the fairies ate and drank, laughed and sang as if no human eye saw them. Immediately behind the throne he stopped and raised himself with his hat in his hand, to catch the whole royal dais under it as a boy catches a butterfly. As he raised himself he suddenly saw that every eye of those thousands was fixed on him. But his greed was stronger than his fear, and he was darting down his hat when a single whistle rang out, and he found his arm caught as if by a thousand strings.

The lights flickered out. The miser rolled to the ground, and felt himself held to it tightly by the threads drawn over him. With a sound like the buzzing of a swarm of bees the fairies were over him, pricking and pinching. He was in agony; but he could neither move nor cry out. The tallest of the Spriggans began a triumphant dance upon his nose. But the moon was paling. At last a cry arose among his tormentors and was taken up by all of them: 'Away, away! I smell the day!' And in a moment they all vanished. When the sun rose the miser found himself lying on the dewy grass, covered with thousands of threads of gossamer. He broke them easily enough, and hobbled down the Gump, aching in every limb. At first he told no one of what had happened to him; but as he grew older he told one or two cronies, and the story has served as a warning to the covetous ever since.

PARALLEL STORIES: There are several stories of thefts of fairy possessions, some of them successful, such as the story of 'The Fairy Cup of the Macleods' and 'The Luck of Edenhall'. More like this is the story of 'Elidor and the Golden Cup', told by Ritson.

AT one of the farms in St. Burien there was a cow called Daisy who always seemed in fine condition. She held her milk from calf to calf, and it was very good milk she gave, but she never gave more than a gallon or so. Her udders would seem full and her milk in full flow when suddenly she would prick her ears and give a gentle low and keep in her milk. The farmer and his wife did not know what to make of it. But one summer evening, when the cows were milked in the meadows, the dairymaid was later than usual, so that the sun was down before she had finished milking Daisy, and turned home with the full pail. To make it softer to her head she plucked a thick wad of meadow

grass, and put it under the pail. As she did so she glanced back, and stood in astonishment, for Daisy was surrounded by a swarm of Little People. One of them, a little larger than the others, was a pixy she was

[1] Hunt, p. 107.

sure, from his impudent grin. He was lying on his back
with his feet in the air, and the others scrambled one
by one on his feet, and milked Daisy into their tiny
pipkins. There were hundreds swarming up her tail
and over her back. They stroked her and whispered
in her ears. The prettiest thing of all was to see how
Daisy enjoyed their company.

The girl hurried home to tell her mistress, who
would not believe a word of it unless they found a
four-leafed clover in the wad of grass. They searched
through it by the light of the lantern, and at length
found one piece of four-leafed clover among the rest.
Then the mistress was convinced; for she knew that a
piece of four-leafed clover on the head gives the power
to see the fairies.

You would have thought that the farmer's wife
would have been content now that she had learned
the truth, for no other farm near flourished as theirs
did; but she was one of those foolish, notable women,
who will never be content to have one drop of gain
spilling abroad; so she went to her mother to find out
how Daisy's milk could be kept for her own use and
away from the fairies. Her mother was a well-known
witch, and as saving as herself. She told her that the
fairies can never endure the smell of fish or fat or brine.
So the farmer's wife boiled a piece of stock fish in a
strong brine and rubbed Daisy's udders with the
broth.

She had her wish, foolish woman; the fairies did not
draw Daisy's milk again, but the poor thing went
about lowing pitifully as if she had lost her calf,
and pined away until they were glad to sell her.

We may hope that the fairies took to her again under her new owner; but at least they left the Farm of St. Burien's, and all its unusual prosperity went with them.

The Gudewife's Midnight Labours[1]

There was once a gudewife who was so stirring and notable that she would rest neither by night nor by day. In the daytime when the meals were cooked and the house was redded up and the animals fed she would wander about and gather wisps of wool caught on the brambles, and at night she would card them and spin them and weave them, and make them up into coats for her man and the bairns. But it was weary work; and one night, as she sat up long after everyone was abed, she threw down her spindle and cried out: 'Ahone, but I'm weary. A body may card, card, card, spin, spin, spin, all day and all night, and what thanks will she get, or help? I'm sure I'd be willing enough to take help from any living thing.'

It was a foolish thing to say, for trouble may always be had for the asking. The words were hardly out of her mouth when there was a knock on the door. The gudewife went to open it, and outside stood the queerest wee body with a green gown and a white mutch.

'Save us! Who's there?' said the gudewife.

'Tall Quarry, gudewife,' said the old woman. 'While I hae ye'll get.' And she crossed over to the fire and began to card. There was another knock, and the gudewife cried out: 'Who's there?'

'Tall Quarry,' said another voice. 'While I hae ye'll get.' And another old woman like the first came in and began to spin. She had hardly started when a third came, who made the same reply and settled down

[1] Elizabeth Grierson, *Scottish Fairy Tales*.

73

to weave. The gudewife was watching them in some alarm when the door opened again, and a fairy boy came in, followed by such a swarm that you might have thought that all the fairies in Scotland were there. They carded and span and wove and boiled the cloth in the fulling pot like mad; and the house was full of the racket of them. For if they had hands they had mouths as well, and all the time they worked they clamoured for food. The gudewife ran to bake bannocks for them, but as fast as one was cooked it was snatched off the fire, and still the clamour went on. At length the gudewife left her cookery and ran to ask her husband what she should do. To her horror he lay like a log, and, shake him as she might, she could not waken him. It was plain that he was bewitched. The gudewife was at her wits end until she thought of consulting a Wise Man who lived near. She pulled her shawl over her head and hurried out to his house. Luckily the Wise Man was but just gone to bed; and he thrust his head out of the window and listened to her story.

'Aweel, there's but one thing to do,' he said. 'If the Good Neighbours have been fulling throw the fulling water over him and he'll maybe waken. But you must get them out from the house first, and syne keep them out. Go back, and as ye come up to the door cry out: "The Burg Hill is afire"! That's where they stay, ye ken. And they'll run out to save what they value most. But mind this, it's of no use to turn them out if ye canna keep them out; so undo all that they've done, or the things they have worked on will rise and open to them.'

The gudewife thanked the Wise Man, and ran as fast as she could to her own house. She flung the door open and cried out: 'The Burg Hill's afire! The Burg Hill's afire!'

At once there was a great clatter and clamour, and the Good People swarmed past her, each crying out the name of his most prized possession. No sooner had they gone than the gudewife slammed to the door, and began to destroy every trace of their work. She pulled the fulling water off the fire and tore the web of cloth, loosed the band of the spinning wheel and turned the distaff upside down, burnt the carded wool and put the cardens in the press. She had barely finished when the fairies knocked at the door.

'Let us in, gudewife. While we get ye'll hae.'

'That I'll not,' said the gudewife. 'Once is enough for this while.'

'Wheel that we spun on,' cried the fairies through the keyhole. 'Rise and let us in.'

A squeaking, wheezy voice came from the spinning wheel. 'I canna let ye in, for the gudewife's lowsed my band.'

'Cardens, cardens, rise and let us in,' said the fairies again, and a small hoarse voice said: 'Hoo can I rise when she's locked me in the press and pit ma wool on the fire?'

'Loom that we worked on, rise up and let us in,' they cried again, and a soft, tongueless voice said: 'Hoo can ye ask me tae rise when my web's torn and my heddle's lying on the ground?'

At that the gudewife laughed, and the fairies cried out: 'Bannocks that we baked, rise up and let us in.'

The gudewife gave a shriek, for she had forgotten the bannocks. There was one little barley bannock cooking on the fire, the last the fairies had set there, and it got up and began to roll towards the door. But the gudewife nipped it between her finger and thumb, and it fell to the ground, for it was but half baked. At that the fairies cried out tauntingly:

'Aha, gudewife, look till yir man! Ye'll no get yir man to waken!'

Sure enough, as they cried out the gudeman began to toss and mutter like one mad. The gudewife wrung her hands again; then she remembered the Wise Man's counsel, and ran to fetch the fulling water. As she dashed the water over her husband the fairies all about the house set up a dismal cry and fled, and the man wakened as well as he had ever been. As for the gudewife, she was careful, after this, never to wish for a thing unless she knew what she was wishing for.

PARALLEL STORY: 'The Horned Women' from Lady Wilde's *Ancient Legends of Ireland*. Campbell has a fragment of a tale in which he gives the fairies' song for their possessions.

Rhys at the Fairy Dance [1]

Two farm servants, Rhys and Llewellyn, had been carrying lime for their master all day, and were returning home with their string of pack ponies when suddenly Rhys stopped.

'Listen to that!' he said. 'I know that tune. It's the best in the world for dancing to, and I'll dance to it before I go a step further.'

'There's nothing,' said Llewellyn. 'I don't hear a sound at all. Come on now. We must get back with the ponies.'

'You go on with the ponies and I'll be after you in a minute,' said Rhys, and slipped away in the dusk.

Llewellyn thought he had made an excuse to get off to the ale-house; so he went slowly on, waiting for Rhys to catch him up. When he got in to his supper the farmer asked where Rhys was, but Llewellyn was a good-natured man and he did not wish to get Rhys into trouble, so he answered vaguely, and sat down to his supper. But Rhys never came that night nor next morning nor the night after that. They searched for him all over the countryside, but found no trace anywhere, and at length the farmer remembered Llewellyn's vague replies, and it began to be said that Llewellyn had killed Rhys and hidden his body, or buried it under the lime. There was no evidence against him, but he had nothing to say for himself that anybody believed, and it would have gone hard with

[1] Keightley, p. 415.

him, but that there was one farmer in the district who knew more about these things than the rest, and from what Llewellyn told him he began to suspect that the Twlwyth Teg might have a hand in this. He suggested to the neighbours that a few of them might go with poor Llewellyn to the place where he had last seen Rhys, and so give him a chance of clearing himself. Half a dozen were ready enough to go; they loosed Llewellyn from the jail and went with him. Sure enough, when they got to the place they found a circle of bright green grass.

'Here's where I saw him last,' said Llewellyn, and then he suddenly cried out: 'What sweet music! I never heard the like before!'

The neighbours looked at each other and shook their heads, but the wise farmer smiled.

'Put your foot on mine, David,' said Llewellyn to one of them, 'and then you'll hear what I hear.'

Sure enough whoever put the point of his toe even over the bright green edge of the fairy ring heard music, like the playing of sweet harps in the distance; and when they leaned a little forward they could see into the ring. It was about twenty feet across, and was filled with little people of the size of three-year children, and all dancing merrily. Rhys was amongst them, laughing and capering, but worn to skin and bone. As he passed near, Llewellyn reached into the circle and pulled him out.

'Where are the horses?' he said wildly.

'Horses!' said Llewellyn. 'We've more to do than to think of horses. Come home with me.'

So Llewellyn's name was cleared, and they took

78

Rhys home. But he was so worn and thin that he had no more strength in him, and soon he took to his bed and died. And the morning after, the fairy ring was stained red with little spots, for all the world like drops of blood. And all over the grass was trodden down with the marks of tiny heels.

PARALLEL STORIES: 'The Farmer and the Tylwyth Teg'; 'Twm and Iago'; 'Taffy ap Sion', from Sikes.

THE STOLEN LADY[1]

IT is one of the laws which govern the fairies that if a human being offers to exchange anything he has for anything of theirs they cannot refuse, however bad the bargain may be. John Roy of Glenbroun knew this, and when the time came he used his knowledge to very good effect.

One night when he was up on the hills looking for his cattle, a flight of fairies passed him with something in their midst. They went so swiftly by him that he had no time to look closely at what they carried; but he feared that it might be some unhappy human creature borne away to captivity beneath the knowes. So like a flash he threw his bonnet into the thickest of the swarm, and cried out in Gaelic: 'Mine be yours and yours be mine!'

The fairies gave a cry of rage and scattered, taking with them John Roy's bonnet, and leaving at his feet a human lady in fine white linen. She was between sleep and waking, sick and fevered; but when he had restored her and carried her back to his clachan he could get no word of Gaelic out of her. It was clear she was no Highlander.

His wife was as noble in hospitality as John Roy himself, and they kept the poor lady with them for many years. In that time the lady had learned the Gaelic and John Roy had learned a little English, so that they could talk together. She told him that she

[1] (Highland.) Keightley, p. 391.

came from England and that she had been carried off on her sick bed. John Roy had no hope that her husband would ever search for her, for he knew that the fairies would have left a stock in her bed, which would soon seem to die and be buried.

So the poor lady lived on without hope of ever seeing her own people again, until at last King George sent his redcoats to build new roads all over the Highlands and to civilize the Highlanders whether they would or no. These redcoats were little liked, as you may imagine, and it was difficult for them to find any lodging; but John Roy had taken a kind of liking for the English because of his stolen lady, and he was a hospitable man besides; so he took the Captain and his son into his house. The English lady was stirred to the very heart to hear the English spoken again; and she looked at the two Englishmen as if she could never look away. They too were glad to hear the English spoken so well in so outlandish a part; and the son, after looking at her closely, said to his father:

'Sir, if I did not know that my dear Mother was dead these many years I should say that I saw her here now.'

'Do you say so?' said the lady. 'And if miracles could happen I should say that I saw my little child grown into a man and standing before me.' Then the father broke in and said:

'You are like what my dear wife would have been if these years had passed over her. Do you know where we lived then and what the house was like?'

Then, weeping with joy, she told him, and they fell on each other's necks and wept together and went over every particular of their parting and her rescue by good John Roy. So the poor stolen lady was restored to her husband; and they all remembered their gratitude to John Roy for as long as they lived.

PARALLEL: 'The Smith and the Woman carried away by Fairies', Irish.

C. HOMELY FAIRIES

THE Homely Fairies may be only the Trooping Fairies seen in their family groups, or they may be the common people of fairyland who do not go to court. They differ from the Heroic Fairies in their homely and prosaic occupations and in their comparatively unsociable habits. They perform the same labours as men, only with tiny tools. Their gifts are not ships that move over land and water, nor cloaks of darkness, nor wishing rings, but loaves of bread and little cakes and sometimes a silver sixpence. Some of them possess the power of invisibility and use a magic ointment which gives second sight, like that in the story of the 'Fairy Midwife' and 'Cherry of Zennor'. This ointment can be made by witches as well as by fairies. These are a mischievous and thieving lot. Others are honest little fellows, good neighbours and with no special powers, though they seem always able to bring good luck.

I have put in this class too the little solitary impets and fairies of the Rumpelstiltzkin type, who will help men in their miraculous tasks, but at a price. The best known of these English fairies is Tom Tit Tot,[1] whose story is so well known that I have not included it. Tom Tit Tot spread even into Wales with the name 'Trwtyn a Trotyn', and into Cornwall, where the droll of 'Duffy and the Devil Terrytop' is almost the same story. The Scottish variant of 'Whuppity Stoorie' is less well known. The heroine here is a widow woman, the task is the cure of her pig and the fairy demands her child as a reward, but the story is substantially the same. Habetrot begins as if it belonged to the same class, but the fairy is a kinder one, and the story turns aside to the plot of Grimm's 'Three Spinners'.

Habetrot is one of the industrious, self-supporting fairies, not domesticated to human hearths like the brownie but supporting themselves by their labours. The leprechauns and cluricans are of this type. Habetrot, however, is a little different from the others, for she is the Queen of the spinning fairies and the patroness of fine spinners upon earth.

Possibly to this class, too, belong those stray fairies who meet wanderers with testing questions. The situation is common, but the characters vary strangely. The Little Grey Man who met the Simpleton in 'The Golden Goose', the Three Golden Heads in the Well, the Goddess Hera whom Jason carried over the

[1] *Folk Lore Journal*, vol. VII, and Jacobs.

river, the woman who met Jesper[1] and gave him the magic whistle — they have little in common except that they all had a favour to ask. As a rule it is wisest to grant favours asked in fairy tales; though Sinbad found to his cost that this is not an invariable rule.

[1] Scandinavian story.

STORIES

CHERRY OF ZENNOR[1]

THERE was once a poor girl called Cherry, one of a family of ten who lived in Zennor, who was determined to see something of the world, so she set out to seek her fortune in service. She tied up her little bundle one fine morning and set out stoutly towards Gerloval. But when the chimneys of Towednack had disappeared behind her her heart began to fail; and when she reached the cross-roads on the Lady Downs she sat down and cried.

At last she said to herself: 'I've no heart for foreign parts. I must just go home again; though I don't know what they'll say to me when I get back.'

With that she raised her eyes, and there was a handsome, dapper gentleman standing beside her, though she didn't know by which of the four roads he had got there.

He gave her good-morning and asked her the road to Towednack; and from that they fell into talk, and Cherry told him how she had set out to find work that morning, and did not know whether to turn back or to go on, for her heart failed her for both.

'This is a bit of luck for me!' said the strange gentleman. 'I set out this morning to find an honest, civil girl to mind my house and look after my orphan

[1] Hunt, p. 120.

child, for I'm a widower. It seems I won't have to go as far as Towednack. If your answers match your looks you're the very girl for me.'

He asked her a few more questions, and praised her well-washed, neatly darned clothes, and engaged her. Cherry was ready enough to go with him, for she had never seen such a sweet-smiling, well-spoken gentleman, and they set out together. It was a long, long road they went; but Cherry's master talked so kindly that she never noticed the way they went, nor how long they were on it. She only knew that they went through narrow, winding lanes, so arched over with trees that the sun hardly  shone into them. At length they came to a rapid stream as clear as crystal; and here the gentleman lifted Cherry and carried her across, so that her feet never touched the water. Then the lane grew twistier and darker and steeper, down and down, till Cherry was quite frightened; but she held her new master's arm and he talked away to her, so that she thought she would go anywhere with so kind a gentleman.

They came at last to a gate in a high wall, and the gentleman unlocked it, and led Cherry into the finest

garden in the world. All kinds of flowers were bloom-
ing at once, all kinds of fruit were hanging ripe upon
the branches, and the birds were singing as Cherry
had never heard them sing before. A little quaint,
sly-looking boy came running out into the garden,
calling: 'Papa! Papa!' and he was followed by a
wizened, cross-grained old woman, who seized him by
the arm and dragged him into the house.

'Never mind her,' said the gentleman. 'She's my
wife's grandmother — Aunt Prudence, she's called.
But she's old and cross and ugly. She'll only stay to
show you the ways of the place and then she's going.'

So Cherry went into the house and ate a grand meal,
and then Aunt Prudence showed her up into the attic
where she was to sleep with the little boy, and warned
her to ask no questions, and to keep her eyes shut,
whatever strange sounds she might hear. Cherry was
full of curiosity, and began to question the child
when they were left alone together; but he soon
stopped her by saying 'I'll tell Granny,' and she had
to go to sleep still puzzled.

She found more things to puzzle her next day, for
some of her duties were very odd. The first thing she
had to do in the morning was to take the little boy out
to a spring in the garden and bathe his eyes and anoint
them with an ointment from a box. But she was to be
very careful to avoid touching her own eyes with the
ointment. She was then to milk the cow. There was
no cow to be seen; but the little boy told her to call one,
and as soon as she called a beautiful little cow pushed
its way through the bushes and stood still to be milked.
The work was light enough, and when it was finished

she went to help her master in the garden. She liked this better than anything, for they got on famously together, and at the end of every row of weeding her master gave her a kiss.

But Aunt Prudence got crosser every day. Nothing that Cherry could do would please her; and in the evenings she sat grumbling to herself that she knew Robin would bring a fool home with him from Towednack. On the fourth day she took Cherry to the shut-up part of the house. They went along a long, dark passage, and then she made Cherry take off her shoes and led her into a fine, grand room with a floor as slippery as glass. All round the walls were stone statues, some busts and some whole figures. Cherry, who had never seen anything of the kind before, was frightened, for she thought the statues were people turned to stone; but Aunt Prudence laughed at her for a fool, and told her to polish up a big six-sided coffer of shining wood. Cherry began very gingerly, but Aunt Prudence scolded her for a coward, and as she rubbed harder she gave the box a kind of push and it groaned so that Cherry fell down in a fit. Her master came running into the room and carried Cherry back to the kitchen, where he revived her tenderly, and sent Aunt Prudence away for giving her such a fright.

After this Cherry was mistress of the house, with no one to find fault with her, and she was so happy that the year flashed by like a week. She and her master grew more and more fond of each other, and Cherry's only grief was that he went away now and then for several days, and when he came back he would go into the gallery of statues, from which Cherry could sometimes hear voices coming, though her master was supposed to be alone. At length this made her so curious that she resolved to find out about it as best she could. She had often noticed that her little charge's eyes were sharper than hers, and even fancied sometimes that she saw him watching things that she could not see, and she wondered if his ointment could give special power to his eyes. So one day when she had anointed him, she sent him to pick some flowers, and slyly put a crumb of the ointment into one of her eyes. It smarted like fire, and she ran to the spring to bathe it. As she knelt down she looked into the water, and there she saw crowds of little lords and ladies, and her master among them, as tiny as any of them and as much at home. She turned aside her eyes, and now she saw every place crowded with the little people. They were singing and dancing everywhere. Cherry was clever enough, however, to say nothing of it to her charge when he came back with the flowers. Presently her master came back and went into the Gallery. Cherry followed him and looked through the keyhole. All the marble people were moving and talking. As Cherry watched, the six-sided box opened and a most beautiful lady came out of it. She sat down and played on her box as if it had been an organ, and when the music stopped Cherry's master bent over and kissed her. At this Cherry burst into tears and ran away crying. When her master came and called her to weed she was sulky and silent. At the end of a row he put an arm round her to kiss her, but Cherry felt this to be too much. She slapped him.

'Get along with you and kiss your little midgets at

the bottom of the spring!' she said. 'But leave me alone!'

Cherry's master looked very grave.

'Oh, Cherry!' he said. 'Have you been putting the ointment on your eyes? You must go, my girl. I'm sad to part with you, but I warned you never to do it. Aunt Prudence must come back again.'

Cherry cried and cried, but there was no help for it. Her master gave her a fine bundle of new clothes, and took her by the hand and led her out of the garden. They walked and walked through the twisting passages and narrow lanes until they came out on to the Lady Downs at daybreak.

'We must part, Cherry,' he said, 'through your fault, not through mine. But if you are a good girl I will come back sometimes to the Lady Downs to see you.'

He left her, and she went weeping home. Her parents were amazed to see her and to hear her strange tale. She never would go to service again, but stayed all her days in Zennor, and her only pleasure was to wander about the Lady Downs in the hope of meeting her kind master once more.

PARALLEL STORIES: 'The Fairy Widower', Hunt; 'The Demon Master', Sikes.

The Fairy Midwife[1]

A WESTMORLAND howdie was summoned one night to go quickly and in great secrecy to an unknown place. She was frightened to go at first, especially as she was told that she must be blindfolded, but the messenger promised her a large reward, and at length persuaded her to mount behind him on a swift horse. She felt herself rushing through the air, and was soon lifted down and led into a cottage, where the bandage was taken off her eyes. She found herself in a decent, clean cottage, with her patient lying on a straw pallet, an old woman attending her, and one or two children about.

In due time a fine baby was born, and the old nurse gave the howdie a pot of ointment, and told her to rub it over the child, but not to touch herself with it. The howdie obeyed, but suddenly one of her eyes itched, and without thinking she raised her right hand, all sticky with the ointment, and rubbed her eye with it. When she looked round the change was so great that she almost dropped the baby. She was no longer in a cottage, but under the large branches of a great hollow oak. The child on her knee was a pointy-eared, bright-eyed elf; the lamp was a cluster of glow-worms; the children were little fairies. But with great presence of mind she kept back her cry of surprise and gave no sign of what she saw. She was rewarded, blindfolded and taken home. And so the matter might have ended; but on the next market day, when she went to town,

[1] Keightley, p. 311.

she suddenly caught sight of the old nurse, busily scraping the pats of butter on the stalls, and putting her scrapings into a jar which hung by her side. As she was looking the nurse raised her head and their eyes met.

'Which eye do you see me with?' said the old woman, coming up to her.

The howdie shut one eye and found that she could no longer see her.

'Why, with this,' she said innocently.

At that the old woman puffed into her eye; and she was blind in that eye for ever, and could never see the fairies again.

PARALLEL STORIES: 'The Pixy Labour', Keightley; 'The Fairy Ointment', Hunt; 'How Joan Lost the Sight of her Eye', Hunt; 'The Fairy Nurseling', Keightley; 'Nursing a Fairy', Hunt; 'The Dracae', Scott's *Minstrelsy of the Scottish Border*; 'The Midwife of Nanhwynan', Rhys.

THE BORROWING FAIRIES[1]

THE Worcestershire fairies are busy little people, ready to help their mortal neighbours or accept help from them. They say that in the old days any woman who had broken her peel, or baking shovel, had only to leave it at the Fairies' Cave in Osebury Rock, and it would be mended when she came for it again. These fairies have even no fear of cold iron, for once a fairy came up to a man ploughing near Osebury, and said:

> 'O, lend a hammer and a nail,
> Which we want to mend our pail.'

and was much delighted by the loan. Again a man who was working near Upton Sudbury suddenly heard a shrill voice crying out in the next field: 'I have broke my bilk! I have broke my bilk!'

At that the man picked up a hammer and nails which he had by him, and went into the next field. There he found a little fairy, lamenting and wringing its hands over its broken bilk, which is a kind of cross-barred stool. He knelt down and mended the stool whilst the fairy danced round him for joy. At length it led him down into a cave, and rewarded him with biscuits and wine, such as he had never tasted before. And from that day, it is said, everything he set his hand to prospered.

PARALLEL STORIES: 'The Fairies' Caldron', Keightley; 'The Fairy Child and the Staff', Sikes.

[1] Jabez Allies, *The Antiquities and Folk Lore of Worcestershire*; quoted in *English Fairy and Folk Tales*, p. 89.

SKILLYWIDDEN[1]

ONE day a farmer was cutting furze on Trendrean Hill near Zennor when he found a little fairy boy, about a foot high, asleep on a bank of heather. He took off his furze cuff, and slipped the little fellow into it without waking him and hurried home. When the little fairy waked up he found himself on the farmer's hearthrug, with the big human children looking at him. He was startled at first, but soon began to peer about, and play with the children, who thought him the best plaything they had ever seen. They called him Bobby Griglans after the place where he had been found, for they call heather griglans in those parts.

Not long after Bobby Griglans was caught the neighbours came for their yearly party to carry home the winter's store of furze. The farmer did not want any of them to catch sight of Bobby, for he hoped to learn from him where the fairy pots of gold were hidden, and he did not want the children's talk to give away what he had found. So the children and Bobby were shut together into the barn while the neighbours had their dinner. But they did not stay

[1] Hunt, p. 450.

95

there long; for presently Bob piped up with a suggestion that they should go and play together round the furze rick. They all scrambled out, and were playing merrily about when they saw a little man and woman, not much bigger than Bob, peering everywhere about the rick. The little woman was ringing her hands and crying out:

'Oh my dear and tender Skillywidden, wherever can'st ah be gone to? Shall I never cast eyes on thee again?'

'Go ee back,' said the little fairy. 'My father and mother are come here too. Here I am, mammy dear!'

With that, Skillywidden and his father and mother were gone from the children's eyes, and they had to turn back to the barn alone.

PARALLEL STORY: 'Colman Grey'.

THE LAIRD O' CO [1]

THE Laird o' Co, as the Lairds of Colzean in Ayrshire were called, was one day returning from a ride round his lands. Near the castle gate he met a very small boy with a wooden tankard in his hands, who begged a drink for his old mother, who was ill. The Laird did not know the child, but he was a good-natured man, and he told the boy to go to the butler and tell him to fill his tankard. The butler had a half empty barrel of ale on tap, and he turned it on. But though the ale ran and ran into the tankard the tankard stayed half full. The butler thought half a tankard was enough for the wee boy's mother, but the wee boy would not go.

'The Laird says it's to be fu',' he said. 'And ye maun fill it.'

At length the butler sent to ask the Laird what he was to do.

'Broach the next cask, man,' said the Laird. 'I promised the wee laddie his can should be filled, and filled it shall be.'

So the butler broached the second

[1] Chambers, *Popular Rhymes of Scotland*, p. 332.

cask, and at the first drop the tankard was full, and the wee boy went with many thanks.

Some years afterwards the Laird o' Co went to the Wars in the Low Countries, where he was taken prisoner and condemned to death. The last night came before the day of his execution, and he was lying in a deep and strong dungeon, without hope, when suddenly the door flew open. The Laird looked up, blinded by the blaze of strong light that shone in, and from out of it he heard a Scotch voice saying:

> 'Laird o' Co,
> Rise and go.'

He got to his feet and came nearer, and as he did so he saw the wee small boy, whose tankard he had filled years ago outside Colzean Castle. The wee boy led him by the hand, and they made their way unchallenged out of the prison. Outside the wee boy made him mount on his shoulders, and in a moment the Laird found himself outside his own castle gate.

> 'Ae guid turn deserves anither,
> Tak ye that for being kind to ma mither,'

said the wee boy: and he vanished out of sight and the Laird o' Co never saw him again.

PARALLEL STORIES: 'Sir Godfrey Macullock', Scott's *Minstrelsy of the Scottish Border*; 'The Farmer of Deunant', Rhys, *Celtic Folklore*.

Tops and Bottoms[1]

THERE was once a Bogie who laid claim to a field on a certain farm. The farmer paid the rent on it, and he saw no reason why another should get the profit; so, after a long argument they agreed that they would part the yield between them, though the farmer should do the work. So the first year at seed time the farmer said: 'Well, mate, which do you choose this year, tops or bottoms?'

'Bottoms,' said the Bogie; so the farmer planted wheat.

At harvest the poor Bogie had nothing but stubble and roots.

'I'll have tops next time,' he said. So the next year the farmer planted turnips.

The Bogie saw that he was getting the worst of the bargain, so he said: 'Next year you'll plant wheat, and we'll have a mowing match, and the one as can mow the biggest part of the meadow shall keep it for ever.'

The farmer agreed; but he knew that the Bogie was likely to be a quicker mower than any living man. So when the corn was growing tall he had a great many iron rods made, and stuck them all about the end of the field where the Bogie would start to mow. The day came, and they hadn't been mowing half an hour when the Bogie's scythe was as blunt as a bone. It is against the rules of a mowing match for one man to whet his scythe before his opponent does; so the Bogie

[1] T. Sternberg, *Dialect and Folk Lore of Northamptonshire*, p. 140.

called to the farmer, who was mowing away in grand style:

'When do we wiffle-waffle, mate?' he said.

'Wiffle-waffle?' said the Farmer. 'Oh, at noon, mebbe.'

'Then I've lost the field!' said the Bogie with a howl of despair; and the farmer was never troubled by him again.

HABETROT[1]

THERE was once a Selkirkshire lassie who was so idle that her mother could never teach her to spin. She was a merry, pretty lass, but her delight was to scramble about in the woods and hills and sit by the burns; and though her mother begged and scolded, she could never get her to sit long enough at her wheel to do any good there. At last her mother lost patience, and she took seven heads of lint and gave them to the lassie.

'See here, ye idle cuttie,' she said. 'Ye'll spin these se'en heids into yarn in three days or I'll gie ye a skelping ye'll no forget.'

The lassie knew her mother meant what she said, and she sat down to work. Her soft little hands were blistered with the harsh lint and her lips were quite sore with licking the thread; but for two days she worked hard and had finished just half a head. She cried herself to sleep that night, for she knew she could never finish the rest of her task in one day; so the next morning she gave it up, and went out into the sunshine and clear air. She wandered up and she wandered down until she came to a little knoll with a stream running past it, and by the stream, sitting on a self-bored stone was an old woman spinning. She looked up as the lassie came up, and her looks were friendly enough, but her lips were so long and thick that the lassie had never seen the like. The lassie smiled at her and came up.

[1] Henderson, p. 221.

'Gude day to ye, gudewife,' she said. 'Ye're a grand spinner, but what way are ye sae lang-lippit?'

'Spinnin' the thread, ma hinnie,' said the old woman kindly.

'I sud be daein' that tae,' said the lassie. 'But it's to nae purpose, a canna dae't in the time.'

'Fetch me yir lint, ma hinnie, and I'll spin it for ye,' said the old wife. The lassie ran away to fetch it, and brought it gladly back.

'Whaur'll I get it again?' she said. 'And what sall I ca' ye, gudewife?' But the old wifie said nothing, but flitted away among the birches faster than you could expect. The lassie wandered up and down the knoll singing to herself; but at last she got sleepy, and sat down on the knoll to sleep. When she wakened the sun had set, and the clear moon was shining down on to her. She had lain down with her head resting on a self-bored stone; and as she was just wondering where she would get her lint again she heard a voice from under her head saying: 'Little kens the wee lassie on the brae head that ma name's Habetrot.'

She put her eye to the bore in the stone and saw right through into the knoll beneath her. It was like a deep cavern, full of spinners, and her friend Habetrot was walking up and down amongst them, watching their work. There was not one among them whose lips were not long and thick like hers. One was sitting a little apart, reeling the yarn, and she was the ugliest of them all, for she had long, thick lips and grey, starting eyes, and a big, hooked nose. Habetrot came up to her.

'Mak' haste noo, Scantlie Meg,' she said. 'That's

ma wee lassie's yarn, and I maun hae it ready to gie her as she gaes into her mither's door.'

The lassie was glad to hear that, for she knew now where she was to wait for the yarn. So she set out for home, and on the doorstep Habetrot was waiting for her. The lassie thanked her gratefully, and asked what she could do for her in return.

'Nocht ava,' said the kind fairy. 'But dinna tell yir minnie wha spinned the yarn.'

It was late now, and the lassie slipped quietly into the house, for her mother was abed. On the table lay seven black puddings which she had made while her daughter was wandering. The lassie had had nothing to eat all day long, and she was hungry; so she blew up the fire again and fired the puddings and ate them, one after the other, until she had eaten all seven. Then she went to bed and slept with an easy heart.

Early next morning the gudewife came down. There on the table were seven beautiful smooth skeins of yarn, but there was no trace of the black puddings except a little burning of the frying pan. At the sight the gudewife was nearly out of her head with vexation and delight; and she ran out of the house, exclaiming:

'My daughter's spun se'en, se'en, se'en,
My daughter's eaten se'en, se'en, se'en,
And all before daylicht!'

The laird was riding by early to the hunt, and he heard her crying out like a mad thing.

'What is it ye're saying, gudewife?' he said.

'My daughter's spun se'en, se'en, se'en.
My daughter's eaten se'en, se'en, se'en,'

said the gudewife again. 'And if ye dinna believe me, Laird, come ben and see for yirsel'.'

The laird came in, and there were seven smooth skeins, and there was the pretty lass, all rosy and fresh from sleep; and he was so taken with her that he asked her to marry him. She was ready enough; but when the wedding was over, and the bridegroom began to talk of the fine yarn she would spin him, her heart failed her, for she could not bear to disappoint him. So she turned it over this way and that in her mind, and at last she went to the self-bored stone, and called on Habetrot by name to come and advise her.

'Bring yir man here, at the full moon, ma hinnie,' said Habetrot, 'and I'se warrant he'll no ask ye tae spin again.'

So when the moon was full the lassie brought the laird to the self-bored stone, and, leaning their ears to it, they heard Habetrot singing. At the end of the song she got up, and, opening a door in the roots of a tree, she called them both in. They went up and down among the rows of spinners, and each one looked uglier than the last.

'They're an unco sicht,' said the Laird at last in a low voice. 'Hoo is it they're sae lang-lippit, gudewife?'

'Wi' spinning, Laird, wi' spinnin',' said Habetrot. 'The bonniest mooth in the warld gets a sair twist to it wi' pu'in' oot the thread.'

'Then we'll hae nae mair spinnin' for ye, ma dearie,' said the Laird. 'Dae ye hear? Ye maun let the wheel bide.'

'Juist as ye say, gudeman,' said the lass, with her heart dancing within her.

So from that day the lassie rode up and down the country with her husband, and hunted and played with him; and very happy they were. And all the lint on the place was sent to Habetrot to spin.

PARALLEL STORIES: 'The Three Spinners', Grimm; 'The Idle Girl with the Three Aunts', *Irish Fairy and Folk Tales*.

THE WOMAN OF PEACE AND THE KETTLE[1]

THERE was once a herd and his wife who lived near the Fairy Knowe on the Isle of Sanntraigh. A Woman of Peace often came to the door to borrow a kettle from the wife. The wife was always ready to lend it; but as she gave the kettle into her hands she always said a snatch of verse, and this is what she said:

> 'A smith is able to make
> Cold iron hot with coal.
> The due of a kettle is bones,
> And to bring the kettle back whole.'

When she said that the Woman of Peace always brought back the kettle in the evening with a good stock of bones in it to make soup.

But one day it happened that the wife had to go over to the mainland; so she said to her husband: 'If the Woman of Peace comes for the kettle today this is what you must say to her.' And she taught him the rhyme. 'You'll be sure to say it, now?' she said.

'Oh yes, I'll say it,' said her husband.

After his wife had gone the herd sat down by the door to twist a rope out of heather for the thatching of the house. As he was twisting he looked up and saw the Woman of Peace with a dark shadow about her feet. She was uncanny to see, and the man was suddenly frightened, and ran into the house and shut the door. The Woman of Peace came to the door and

---

[1] Campbell.

called; but the herd would not open it. She went calling round the house. When she got to the side where the smoke hole was he heard her clearest, and the kettle gave a little hop on the fire. She called again and again, and the kettle rose up through the smoke hole and went to her, while the man blessed himself that it was no worse.

In the evening the wife came back and looked round for the kettle. There was no sign of it.

'Did the Woman of Peace come for the kettle?' she said. 'And did you say the rhyme to her?'

'Oh, don't speak of her,' said the herd. 'She gave me the fright of my life. She's off with the kettle, and I'm thankful it's no worse.'

'My sorrow!' said his wife. 'You'll be the destruction of us. We'll never get the kettle now.'

'Maybe it will come back tomorrow,' said the herd.

'It will not,' she said, 'unless I fetch it.' And she set off running to the Bruth, as the fairy knowe was called in those parts.

The knoll was open when she got to it, for it was twilight; and the kettle was on the fire, and no one within. So she ran in and picked up the kettle — it was heavy for her to carry for it was full of meat. But there was an old Man of Peace crouching in the room beyond, and as she lifted the kettle he called out to her:

> 'Silent wife, silent wife,
> That came on us from the Land of Chase,
> Thou man on the surface of the Bruth,
> Loose the Black and slip the Fierce!'

She ran all the faster for that, but soon she heard the dogs of Peace baying behind her. She put her hand into the kettle and threw a good handful of meat back to them. The dogs stopped to eat it, but they soon came on. She threw out some more, and they made short work of that. Then she turned the kettle upside down, and emptied all that was in it on the ground. As she ran on the human dogs from the steading came barking out at the dogs of Peace and drove them back. So the wife got safe home with her kettle; but the Woman of Peace never came borrowing again.

THE LEPRECHAUN[1]

TOM FITZPATRICK, a farmer's son who lived near Morristown Luttin, was strolling about one fine autumn day. A saint's day it was, and the fields were empty of workers, when suddenly, behind a hedge a little in front of him he heard a sharp click-clack, click-clack. It was late for a stonechat to be calling, and the sound was hardly like a stonechat either, so Tom stole forward on his tiptoes to see what kind of a beast or bird it might be that was making the noise. His eyes nearly popped out of his head when he saw below him on the shady side of the hedge a little wee man in a cocked hat and a red coat, with a leather apron round his waist, working away at a tiny shoe; the leprechaun, no less. Now Tom knew that every leprechaun has one crock at least of buried gold, and it will be a rich man that can make him give it up. So he stole quietly up till he was within arm's reach of the wee man, and: 'God bless your work, honest man,' says he.

The leprechaun threw him a crooked glance from under his eyebrows; but he said, 'Thank ye kindly,' civilly enough.

'I wonder you'd be working on the holiday,' said Tom.

'I wonder you wouldn't be minding your own business instead of mine,' said the wee man. 'It'd be better for ye to be driving out the cows from your

[1] Keightley, p. 373.

father's oats, where they're knocking the corn about than to be pestering me with questions.' And he pointed to the field of oats behind Tom's back.

But Tom wasn't the one to be caught that way. He stretched out and grabbed hold of the wee man. 'Now,' says he, 'I have ye, and ye'll not get out of my grasp with one limb of ye joined to another without ye tell me where ye've hidden yer gold.' Tom looked so fierce that the wee man was frightened for his life, as well he might be, and he said: 'Follow where I tell ye then, and I'll show ye where there's enough gold hid to put ye past the taste of want for the rest of yer days.'

So he told Tom to go this way and that, and rough, hard ways they were; but Tom never took his eyes off him, for he knew that if he so much as twinkled his eye the leprechaun would be away. At long length they came to a great field, all covered over with the yellow ragwort, as they call the bolyauns in England.

'Now,' said the wee man, 'dig under the root of that tall bolyaun yonder and ye'll find a crock of gold as big as yer head.'

Tom hadn't a fork or shovel with him; so he tied his red garter round the bolyaun to know it again.

'Will ye be wanting me any more?' said the leprechaun.

'No, honest man,' said Tom. 'The gold's all I'm wanting.'

'Then mind and make good use of it,' said the leprechaun, and he slipped away like a drop of water into sand. As for Tom, he ran for his fork as fast as the wind, and in two minutes time he was back. There was the field, twenty good acres of it, and round every bolyaun in it there was a red garter tied, so like Tom's that you could not tell the difference. If he'd dug up the whole field he'd have been digging till Doomsday; so he turned round and went home, and he never saw the leprechaun again from that day to this.

In another story retold by Keightley a woman saw three leprechauns working together. The clurican is very like the leprechaun, but it is fond of getting into cellars and drinking there. Mr. Yeats says that the leprechauns and other Solitary Fairies wear red caps and the Trooping Fairies green. A man in Ireland once saw a fight between red coated and green coated fairies, and he was so glad to see the green coats winning that he let out a shout, and the whole thing vanished from his sight.

PART TWO

THE TUTELARY FAIRIES

THE TUTELARY FAIRIES

THE Tutelary Fairies, perhaps remote descendants of the Lares and Penates, are of two kinds — the ominous and the homely. The banshee is the great example of the first type. Though there are death portents everywhere the banshee — the Fairy Woman who attaches herself to the fortunes of a family and bewails its misfortunes — seems to be peculiarly Celtic. The Irish banshee is described as a tall, pale woman in white, with long teeth and eyes fiery red from weeping. She only attaches herself to the old Milesian stock, and will never wail for newer importations. She can be heard keening and screaming and clapping her hands round a house where a death is to be expected. Lady Fanshawe, in her *Memoirs* written in the seventeenth century, describes an apparition that was evidently the banshee. The banshee of the McCartneys, told by Crofton Croker and quoted in *Irish Fairy and Folk Tales*, is one of the most dramatic of the banshee stories. When a number of banshees wail together it means the death of some great or very holy person.

The Highland banshee is called the Washer by the Ford, or the Little Washer of Sorrow. She sits by a ford, washing the death clothes of the man next to die and keening loudly. Anyone brave enough to catch her can force her not only to tell him the name of the doomed man but to grant her captor a wish. Scott, in his *Demonology and Witchcraft*, mentions a Highland banshee who not only wailed for the dying of her clan but watched over the living, particularly guarding the infant chief in his cradle, and even suggesting moves to the chief when he played chess.

There is a Welsh banshee, Gwrach y Rhibyn, who like the Irish banshee will only take an interest in the old families. She is very hideous, tall and shrivelled with fiery eyes and long yellow teeth. There is also the Cyhyraeth, or groaning spirit, which is never seen, but is heard giving terrifying shrieks and groans. It is not a tutelary spirit attached to any special family, but rather belongs to certain places. Some Cyhyraeths are said only to cry out before the death of innocents or mad men, but in the seaside villages they groan before a shipwreck, and in some places are always heard before an epidemic. There are many stories of the various kinds of banshees, but it is useless to tell them here, for they are not suitable to be re-told to children; so we may proceed to the homelier kind of Tutelary Fairy.

Hobgoblin was formerly a polite title for the friendly domestic fairies; though the word has lately gained rather a sinister sound. This type of fairy is known all over Europe, and appears again and again in both the Celtic and the Saxon Folk Lore of the British Isles.

The brownies are the commonest type of all; but stories occur of a great many other fairies acting much like brownies. The brownie is a small, shaggy spirit dressed in rags; he haunts one special place, into which he comes at night, tidying everything that has been left untidy, but often untidying what has been left tidy. It seems to be a condition of his working for humans that he should get no reward; and a gift of clothes especially will drive him away for ever. Different reasons are given for this. Sometimes it is said that he becomes too proud of his finery to work, sometimes that he goes off to fairyland so soon as he is respectably dressed, sometimes that a doom laid on him is lifted if he is considered to have earned a reward, and yet again that he cannot bear to feel himself the hired servant of mankind. The Phynoderee of the Isle of Man was said to be banished from the Fairy Court for dancing with a human girl, and to be forced to work off his spell in human habitations; and the brownie is often described as the ordained servant of man, mercifully allowed him to lighten the curse of Adam.

On the other hand the brownie is often said to be a ghost, like the Cauld Lad of Hilton, who was supposed to be the ghost of a stable boy, killed in a passion by one of the lords of Hilton. Otherwise, the Cauld Lad behaved exactly like a brownie.

The brownies considered themselves responsible for the welfare of the household to which they were attached, and always kept the servants in strict order, which was one reason of their being often laid. They were occasionally very tricksy; and indeed a boggart seems sometimes merely a brownie in a bad temper.

The brownies were not exclusively domestic. In the Border Country, where people were often forced to bury their goods, the brownie was invoked as the guardian of the hidden treasure. Some kind of ceremony was performed to call him, evidently partly sacrificial, for the blood of a slain animal was spilled on the ground. Where no brownie was to be got the good-natured, stupid dobie often took his place. But he was easily outwitted, and the brownie was much preferred as a guardian. The Highland brownies seem generally to have lived out of doors, often by water, with which brownies of all kinds are closely associated, and only to have come into the house at night. The same thing may be noticed in the Irish story of the Pooka. In the Highlands there is an occasional female brownie. Keightley tells of a household in Tulloch Gorm haunted by two, a male and a female, called Brownie Clod and Hairy Mag. Brownie Clod was much less knowing than his sister, and was a frequent butt of the servants.

Other hobgoblins of the same type are: Billy Blind, Bluecap, the Bodachan Sabhaill, Booman, the Bwbachod, Cowie, the Dobby, the Dobie, Ghillie Dhu, Gruagach, Hob or Hobthrush, Killmoulis, Lob-Lie-by-the-Fire, Luridan, Phynnodderee, the Portunes, Robin Goodfellow, Robin Roundcap, a Silky, the Urisk and Wag-at-the-Wa'. Short particlars of these are given in the 'Dictionary of Fairies' at the end of the book.

The boggart is a hobgoblin like the brownie, but a mischievous one. He behaves exactly like a poltergeist — breaks china, hurls things about, sweeps past invisibly on the stairs with a swish of silk, thumps and dances in empty rooms and answers knock for knock. One story, quoted by Rhys in *Celtic Folk Lore*, tells of a Welsh Bwca who sank from a brownie into a boggart. I have long known an English version of the same story, almost identical in every particular, whose source I have been unable to trace, but which I give later for what it is worth.

STORIES

THE CAULD LAD OF HILTON [1]

HILTON CASTLE in the valley of the Wear had once its brownie, who was something between a brownie and a ghost. He was said to be the spirit of a stable boy killed by one of the old lords of Hilton; but he played all the usual brownie pranks. At night he would play about the kitchen and throw down all the pots that had been put in order; but if the place was left topsy-turvy he would tidy it. The servants often heard him singing a melancholy song to himself.

> 'Wae's me, wae's me!
> The acorn's not yet
> Fallen from the tree
> That's to grow the wood
> That's to make the cradle
> That's to rock the bairn
> That's to grow to the man
> That's to lay me!'

But his forebodings were too gloomy. In spite of his help in their work the servants found him uncanny company; so they set to work to lay him, and left a green mantle and hood by the fire for him. He put them on and danced about in them, and just before

[1] Keightley, p. 296.

cockcrow they heard him singing. But instead of singing his melancholy 'Wae's me', he sang gaily....

> 'Here's a cloak and here's a hood;
> The Cauld Lad of Hilton will dae nae mair good.'

Then at the first sound of cockcrow he whisked out of the door and was never seen again.

PARALLEL STORIES: This story in some form or another is one of our commonest, and several variants follow.

THE BROWNIE OF JEDBURGH[1]

THERE was a brownie in one of the border keeps near Jedburgh who had a special kindness for the lady of the house. One night she fell suddenly into labour, and the master told one of the menservants to ride at once to Jedburgh for the midwife. But it was a wild night and the fords were high; and, though it was a  matter of life and death, the man dressed slowly and grumblingly. Every moment of delay was perilous, and the brownie could not bear that his friend should be endangered; so he slipped on the servant's greatcoat, mounted the terrified horse, and went like the wind to Jedburgh. The midwife heard a voice calling her down out of the darkness, and went down and mounted, thinking no more than that it was strange that they should have sent so small a boy on such an errand. The horse started back so furiously that she needed all her wits and all her strength to cling on. The river was roaring past them at the ford, and the

[1] Scott, *Minstrelsy of the Scottish Border*.

midwife let out a shriek of horror; but they crossed it safely, and the midwife went up to the lady's room in time to save her life. The brownie left the shivering and exhausted horse in the stable, and went up to the servant's room, whom he found slowly pulling on his second boot. He picked up the horse whip which was lying near and gave the servant a thrashing which he never forgot.

The master of the house heard the story and ordered that a bowl of cream should be set out every night for the brownie. So far so good, but his gratitude went further. Someone heard the brownie say to himself one night — 'Wae's me for a braw green coat', and told the Master of it. The Master did not want to leave a wish of the kind brownie's ungratified, so he had a green coat made and laid out for him. If he had known more of brownies he would have known the result of such a gift. The brownie put on the green coat, danced about and disappeared, never more to be seen near Jedburgh.

This is a typical brownie story. The one which follows is perhaps only interesting as showing how close the resemblance is in different places. There seem to be three recognized ways of laying a brownie — a gift, naming, and exorcism — intentional or not. In the following story the third method is used.

THE NITHSDALE BROWNIE [1]

THERE was a brownie who once haunted the old pool on the Nith, and worked for Maxwell, the Laird of Dalswinton. Of all human creatures he loved best the Laird's daughter, and she had a great friendship for him and told him all her secrets. When she fell in love it was the brownie who helped her and presided over the details of her wedding. And when the pains of motherhood first came on her it was he who fetched the cannie wife. The stable boy had been ordered to ride at once; but the Nith was roaring high in spate and the straightest path had an ill name, for it went through the Auld Pool, so he loitered. The brownie flung his mistress's fur cloak over his shoulders, mounted the best horse while the servant was still dressing and crossed the roaring waters. As they rode back the cannie wife hesitated at the road they came.

'Dinna ride by the Auld Pool,' she said. 'We mecht meet the brownie.'

'Hae nae fear, gudewife,' said he. 'Ye've met a' brownies ye're like to meet.'

With that he plunged into the water and carried her safely over to the other side.

After he had set her down at the Hall steps he went round to the stable, where he found the servant, still putting on his boots. He took the bridle off the horse and thrashed the boy soundly.

This happened soon after the time of the Reforma-

[1] Keightley, p. 357.

tion; and Maxwell of Dalswinton told the Minister the story. The Minister was anxious to baptize so affectionate and zealous a servant. So he hid in the stable with a stoup of holy water; and, as the brownie was beginning his night's work, threw the water over him and began the form of baptism. But he never completed it, for the brownie gave one yell of terror and disappeared. Nor was he seen in Nithsdale again.

THE BROWNIE OF CRANSHAWS [1]

BROWNIES, however well intentioned and industrious, are as touchy as most fairies about careless words. The Brownie of Cranshaws in Berwickshire used to work very hard at harvest time every year, both cutting the corn and thrashing it. You would have thought the servants would have been lastingly grateful to be spared one of their hardest labours; but some people value little what they get easily, and at length one of the servants, going into the barn, called to his fellows: 'The Brownie's nae mair than a Dobie! The corn's no weel mowed nor weel stacked the year.'

Unfortunately, the brownie heard him, as brownies commonly hear most that goes on in a farm, and that night there was a great tramping to and fro in the barn, in and out; and the servants who lay above, but did not dare to go down, heard the brownie muttering to himself as he went out and in:

'It's no weel mowed! It's no weel mowed!
Then it'll ne'er be mowed by me again;
I'll scatter it ower the Raven Stane,
And they'll hae some wark ere it's mowed again.'

In the morning not an ear of corn was to be found in the barn. The brownie had carried it all to Raven's Crag, two miles away, and flung it over. And he never came back to work in Cranshaws again.

PARALLEL STORY: 'The Manx Phynnodderee who was Slighted by the Farmer', Henderson.

[1] Henderson, p. 212.

PUDDLEFOOT[1]

In Altmor Burn near Cloichfoldich a brownie used to live in former times. He came into the house at night and washed and arranged all the dirty dishes left lying about; but if the dishes had been put away he took them all down and threw them on the floor. He was pleased to have milk left out for him, and always left something in exchange. Because of the way he used to come splashing in from the burn the cottagers called him 'Puddlefoot' behind his back; but none dared to speak to him nor cared to pass his pool in Altmor Burn after nightfall. One night, however, a man came drink-valiant back from the market and crossed the burn by the brownie's pool. The brownie was there, splashing about in the water.

'Oh, you're there are you, Puddlefoot?' the man called. The brownie hated the name.

'Oh dear! Oh dear!' he cried. 'I've got a name. They call me Puddlefoot.' And he vanished and never came back again.

PARALLEL STORY: Henderson gives a parallel story with rather a different turn. This is the story of a little ghost. It is believed in Fife that the souls of unnamed children have no standing in the spirit world. One such little one used to wail about the lanes of Whittinghame, crying: 'Nameless me! Nameless me!' up and down the place. No one dared to speak to it for fear of being struck dead. One night,

[1] A story lately current in Perthshire.

however, a drunk man passing through the village heard it wailing, and called out: 'How is't wi' ye the nicht, Shorthoggers?'

Shorthoggers was no more than a nickname,. taken from babies' little woollen boots, but it was name enough for the little ghost. He cried joyfully: 'Oh weel is me noo, I hae gotten a name. They ca' me Short-hoggers of Whittinghame.' And he ran away to join the other spirits and never haunted Whittinghame again.

FROM BROWNIE TO BOGGART [1]

THIS is the sad story of a brownie's fall. Several hundreds of years ago a brownie, who had shifted from house to house, at last settled in a big manor farm where there was a stable boy called Dick with whom he made great friends. He would do anything for Dick, and Dick in his turn always left a sup in the bottom of his bowl for the brownie. So it might have gone on till Dick was an old man; but those were sad, wild times of civil war, and Dick was taken for a soldier and fell fighting at Bosworth Field against Richard Crookback. After that the poor brownie had no friend about the house; and, as a dog will sometimes grow mischievous and morose when it is unhappy, so the brownie gave himself over more and more to mischief until he was no better than a boggart. Indeed, he grew so much of a boggart that he even grew a boggart's long, sharp nose. Sometimes he bewitched the ploughing oxen, so that they followed him wherever he turned, dragging the plough after them, until the field was marked like sand on the seashore, or with figures of eight and broken circles. At night he would smash all the crockery on the dresser, and make such a noise that no one in the house could sleep. Things got worse month by month, and no one could have gone on living in the house if the village cobbler had not come to their help. He was a very learned man and had a

---

[1] Forgotten Source.

book of charms strong enough to lay the worst spirit that ever walked.

The boggart had a favourite dark corner behind the wainscotting where he usually lurked in the daytime. The cobbler rolled up an empty cask to the corner and solemnly laid his magic book upon it. The boggart was full of curiosity, and his long, sharp nose showed suddenly, peering through the crack. Quick as a flash the cobbler seized it between finger and thumb and drove his sharp awl through it, pinning it to the wainscot. The boggart howled and kicked, but the cold iron held him fast. Then the cobbler opened his book, and solemnly read a long conjuration. At the end of it he took out the awl and ordered the boggart into the cask. The boggart, thoroughly cowed, obeyed, and the cobbler shut up the bunghole and imprisoned him inside. Then he started to read from his book again. As he read, a tremendous wind swept into the room and carried away the cask with the boggart in it. And wherever the boggart came down it was too far from his old haunts for him to get back again.

PARALLEL STORIES: Rhys, in his *Celtic Folk Lore*, gives a story so like this as to be identical, except for the name of the stable boy, which was Moses, and some earlier adventures, in one of which we learn that his name was Gwarwyn-a-throt.

A barrel seems to be a favourite vessel for unwanted spirits. It is used to lay the spirit of a former rector in the story told by Henderson about a Dartmoor parsonage.

The Boggart[1]

There was once a Yorkshire farmer called George Gilbertson whose house was much tormented by a boggart. He played his tricks on everyone about the house, and especially on the children. He would snatch away their bread and butter and upset their porringers and shove them into corners and cupboards; and yet not a glimpse of him was ever seen. There was an elf-bore in one of the cupboards, a hole where a knot of wood had been, and one day the youngest boy stuck an old shoehorn into it. It was pushed back so hard that it popped out of the hole and hit him on the forehead. After this the children loved to play with the boggart by thrusting sticks into the hole and seeing them shot back. But the boggart's tricks got worse and worse, and poor Mrs. Gilbertson be- came so anxious for the children that at last they decided to move. So on the day of the flitting their nearest neigh- bour, John Mar- shall, saw them following their last creaking carts out of the empty yard.

[1] Keightley, p. 307.

131

'And so you're flitting at last, Georgie?' he said.

'Aye, Johnny lad, I'm forced tull it; for that domned boggart torments us soa we can neaither rest neet nor day for't. It seems to have sech a malice against t' poor bairns that it omost kills my poor dame at thowt on't. And soa ye see we're forced to flit like.'

A sudden unexpected echo to his words came in a deep voice out of the old upright churn in the last cart.

'Aye, Johnny lad, we're flitting, ye see.'

'It's the domned boggart!' said George. 'If I'd a knowed thou'd been there I hadn't a stirred a leg. Turn back, Mally,' he said to his wife. 'We mun as well be tormented in t'owd house as in another that's not to our liking.'

So back they went; and the boggart played about their farm till he was tired of the sport.

PARALLEL STORY: 'The Welsh Farmer and the Bwbach', Sikes.

THE POOKA

POOKA seems to be the Irish form of Puck, as
Keightley believes leprechaun to be of lubberkin.
Puck and Robin Goodfellow and the Boguey Beast
can all turn themselves into horses, but the Pooka
seems almost always to appear as an animal of some
kind. One story is given in *Irish Fairy and Folk Tales*
of the pooka carrying off an old piper into a fairy hill,
where he gained a magical power of piping, as well
as a set of pipes that made a noise like geese, and this
pooka was something like a horse, but with long horns.
The Kildare pooka was like an ass, however, and
behaved exactly like a brownie. His story is given by
Patrick Kennedy in *Legendary Fictions of the Irish Celts*.

There was a household in Kildare where the servants were often frightened by the sound of splashing
and trampling in the night time. One night it happened that a kitchen boy had fallen asleep by the fire,
and never wakened when the other servants went to
bed. In fact he never wakened till midnight, when the
door opened and a large ass came clattering into the
room. The boy was too frightened to stir, and he
looked on as the ass dragged a big tub into the middle
of the floor, and, picking up the kettle in its teeth, set
it on the fire to boil. Then it sat down by the fire till
the water boiled, and gave a kind of unearthly grin
at the boy. But he was too frightened to say anything,
and the pair of them sat silently there together. Until
cockcrow the pooka toiled away. It put every dish in

the place into the tub, and it washed and polished them all till they shone. It swept up the place and left it like a new pin. Then just before dawn it clattered out, and the boy ran upstairs to tell what he had seen. One said one thing and one said another, but a lazy slut of a housemaid made the greatest hit of all, for she said:

'What's the use of us wearying ourselves with tidying and cleaning when the pooka does it all again? Leave the work, it will be as well pleased.'

Everyone felt this to be good sense, and from this on the house was a paradise to the servants. Choose how they left the place at night — and believe me they never left it tidy — it would be like a new pin in the morning. And so it might have gone on till this day if a busy, curious bit of a boy hadn't chosen to sit up and have his morsel of talk with the pooka.

At twelve o'clock the pooka clattered in and set to work. While he was waiting by the fire for the kettle to boil the boy spoke to him.

'Can ye tell me now, sir, where ye come from, and why ye're willing to do the work for the idle girls every night of their lives?'

'I'll tell ye and welcome,' said the pooka, quite glad of a bit of talk. 'I was a rogue of an idle servant in this house once, as ever ate and drank of the best and did nothing for his keep; and after I died it was laid on me that I must work here for no keep at all half of the night, and half of the night I must stand outside in the bitter cold and wet; and hard enough it is in the winter season like it is at this present.'

'I'm sure and we're obliged to ye,' said the boy, 'for

all ye do for us. Isn't there anything, now, we could do to make it easier to you?'

'I'm obliged to ye,' said the pooka. 'There's one thing would be the greatest comfort in life to me, and that's a good padded coat to cover my back and my four cold legs.'

'Well, I'm sure ye deserve no less,' said the boy. 'And we'll do our best for ye.'

So two nights later the boy was waiting with the padded coat, and a queer looking contraption it was; but between them they got the pooka's four legs into it, and it buttoned under his belly. Then the pooka began to caper about with joy and ran to look at himself in the glass. 'It's a handsome coat ye've given me,' he said. 'Never a pooka had the like. And now I've no call to be minding the wind or the rain or anything at all.' And he made for the door.

'Stop a bit!' said the boy. 'There's all those plates and glasses to be washed before ye go.'

'It's not a one of them I will wash from this time,' said the pooka. 'It was laid on me that I had to work till someone thought that I'd fairly earned a reward. I've earned it now, and the kitchen girls can wash their own dishes from this day on.'

With that it kicked up its heels and out into the darkness with it; and from that day any work that was done in the house was done by the boys and girls, for they had no help from the pooka.

THE KIND PIXY [1]

PIXIES do brownie work sometimes; and there is a story of a kind pixy mentioned by Mrs. Bray and told in more detail in Mrs. Wright's *Rustic Speech and Folk Lore.*

A poor young woman once married a thresher who turned out to be a hopeless drunkard. Day after day he was too drunk for his work; and at last she dressed herself in man's clothes and went to thresh in his place. One morning when she came into the barn she found that twice as much corn had been done as she had left threshed the night before. And so it went on for days. At length the woman determined to watch at night; and when night came she hid in a corner of the barn. Darkness had not long fallen before a tiny, naked pixy crept into the barn, and began threshing with a little flail. He worked and worked, and as he worked he sang:

> 'Little pixy, fair and slim,
> Without a rag to cover him.'

It was no wonder that the woman determined to make him clothes; and she made him a tiny suit and hung it next night in the barn. When he saw it the pixy capered with joy and put it on. Then he danced about singing:

> 'Pixy fine and pixy gay,
> Pixy now must fly away.'

Then he danced out of the barn and never threshed there again.

[1] Mrs. Wright, *Rustic Speech and Folk-Lore,* p. 209.

PART THREE

THE NATURE FAIRIES

THE NATURE FAIRIES

OF the large number of Nature Spirits which must once have peopled this country only very few remain, and those few in a melancholy and debased condition. There are three chief classes of water spirits — the patrons of wild life, the personified forces of Nature, and the localized spirits which haunt particular rocks, waters and woods. Of these the last is far the commonest.

Very few of the first class are left to us. The Welsh Gwyllion perhaps belong to it, though they might rather be placed in the third class. They are the patrons of the mountain goats, whose beards they comb on Wednesdays, the fairies' Sunday. They often take the form of goats. They are dangerous to mankind. In the Border Country the Brown Man of the

Muirs, like them dangerous to mankind, is the protector of the moorland creatures. Others, who may have been gods in their day have dwindled down into the homely forms of Awd Goggie, who protects unripe gooseberries, and Churn-milk Peg and Melch Dick who guard the nut thickets.

Perhaps the only personification of a natural force is the Hag of Winter — Cailleach Bheur she is called in the Highlands, Milton's blue meagre hag, Gentle Annie of Leicester and Black Annis further north. The Cailleach Bheur is withered, meagre and dreadful, with only one eye. Her staff has the power of freezing and death; but in springtime, when the rising sap prevails against it, she throws it petulantly away into a holly bush. This is why no green grows at the root of a holly. Gentle Annie and Black Annis have more connection with the sea than the Cailleach Bheur, and are specially dreadful in raising storms.

Quite a number of the local deities remain, though water has kept its spirits longer than land. We have no wood nymphs, like the German Wood Women or the Swedish Elle People, although there are some faint traces of the Scandinavian Light Elves in such stories as 'The Tulip Fairies'. Our last Dryad belongs to the elder tree. This tree was much revered, and the *Lincolnshire Folk Lore* gives a rhyme in which permission is asked to cut the tree. Wood from a tree cut without permission was most unlucky, particularly for a cradle. Not long ago an Oxfordshire countryman told me with pride that he had often cut elder wood, and it had never bled. It is often a little difficult to differentiate the Nature Fairies from the general

Fairy People. Most of these are mound dwellers, with a good deal of power over fertility, and natural supplies. For instance, the Danaans locked all the wells of Ireland against Conary when he was dying of thirst, many of the Tutelary Fairies have special pools or rocks, such as Hobhole Hob's cave or the Pooka's rock. But the clear-cut numerous Nature Fairies are mostly water spirits. Here are some of them: The Afanc, Aughisky, The Blue Men of the Minch, Crodh Mara, The Dracae, Each Uisge, or the Water Horse, The Fideal, The Ganconers, Grindylow, The Gwragedd Annwn, Jenny Greenteeth, the Kelpie, Llamhigyn y Dwr, the Loireag, Mermaids and Mermen, Merrows, Muileartach, the Neagle, Nuckelavee, Peg Powler, The Plant Annwn, The Roane, Selkies, Shellycoat, Shony, Shoopiltee, Tangie and the Water Wraith. A little about each of these will be found in the 'Dictionary of Fairies' at the end of the book. A few of these water fairies are harmless, like the Seal People, but most are malevolent. One of the most revolting of them is Nuckelavee, of whom a vivid description is given in *Scottish Fairy and Folk Tales*. Perhaps such monsters are best forgotten when telling tales to our youngers; for delicate nerves are often hidden under a bold front. Here are a few adventures by sea and fresh water, impressive, no doubt, but not unduly harrowing. At the end is one land story from among the small number that remain.

STORIES

The Merrow and the Soul Cages[1]

THE female merrows are a lovely sight, with their flowing hair and their white, gleaming arms and their dark eyes; but the male merrows are nothing worth looking at, for they have green hair and green teeth and little pig's eyes and long red noses, and short arms more like flippers than any respectable arm that could do a day's work. For all that there was once one man that was very anxious to see a merrow, and that was Jack Dogherty, that lived with his wife Biddy in a snug little cabin hard by the seashore not far from Ennes. It was the more provoking that Jack could never catch a glimpse of one because his own grandfather had been so chief with a merrow that, if it hadn't been for offending the priest, he'd have asked him to stand godfather to his children; and here was Jack living in the very place and looking out day and night without so much as the glimpse of a fin. At last one day, on a rock about half a mile along the coast, Jack made out a shape of a creature, standing as still as a stone with a thing like a red cocked hat on its head. It stood so still that he almost thought it was a piece of the rock with the sunset on it; when suddenly he gave a sneeze, and the thing plunged into the water, so Jack knew that he had seen a merrow at last. But he was not content with

1 (Irish.) Crofton Croker, p. 194.

142

that. He wanted a word with it; and he hung round the merrow's rock day in, day out, and sometimes he got a glimpse of it; but it was not until the powerful storms set up at the back end of the year that he saw the creature at all close. Then it would play about the rock as fearless as a pike after salmon, and it happened at last one blowy day that Jack got right up to it. And an ugly old fellow it was, with its scaly legs, ending in a bit of a tail, and its finny arms and its long, strong, green teeth. But it rolled a friendly eye at him, and said, just like a Christian: 'Good day to you, Jack Dogherty, and how have you been keeping this while back?'

'Your Honour's very pat with my name,' said Jack, surprised.

'And why wouldn't I know your name?' said the merrow, 'and I like a brother almost with your own grandfather. That was a great man, Jack. There was never a one could put him under the table. I wonder now, do you take after him.'

'I may not take after him all ways,' said Jack. 'But if it's liking liquor and good liquor you mean I'm the very double to him. But I wonder where Your Honour'd get the liquor out of the sea; unless it might be salt water, which isn't to every man's taste.'

'Faith, and where do you get it yourself, Jack?' said the merrow, winking at him.

Now Jack got the most of what he drank and what he sold too out of the sea, for there was many a cask of good wine drifted up out of the Atlantic to his cabin door; and though he'd never have been the one to hurt poor sailors, he thought it no harm to take what they were past wanting and could never use. So Jack winked back at the merrow, and said:

'Oh, I take Your Honour now. But it's a big cellar ye'll be needing and a dry cellar to keep all the sea gives you.'

'So it is then,' said the merrow. 'And if you come to this rock at this time on Monday, we'll go further into the subject.' And with that it turned and dived into the sea.

Next Monday Jack was there for certain; for he didn't mean to lose his chance of making friends with a merrow after all the trouble he'd been at. The merrow was there before him, and he had two cocked hats under his arm instead of one.

'Here's a chance for you now, Jack,' he said. 'I've got a loan of a second hat for you. Put it on, and you shall come and see my cellar, and get a taste of it into the bargain.'

'Thank you, Your Honour,' said Jack. 'But a plain man like me would be drowned plunging down into the sea like a fish.'

'Tush,' said the merrow. 'You're not a quarter what the grandfather was before you. He never stood a minute when he first got the chance to come down and see me.'

'Well, I won't be a worse man than my grandfather,' said Jack, 'so lead on.'

'Well said!' said the merrow. 'Follow me, and hold on to my tail when I go down.'

They swam out straight enough to a rock a little way out, and Jack began to wonder what would happen next, when the merrow said: 'Hold on now!' and down they went; down, down, down, with the water rushing past Jack's head, so that he could neither see nor breathe, and it was all that he could do to hold on. At last they landed bump on to some soft sand, and Jack found he was in air again, as good to breathe as ever he smelt. He looked up, and there was the sea above them, as it might be the sky, and the fishes swimming about over their heads, like the birds flying. In front of them was the merrow's house, with a strong spurt of smoke going up from the chimney. They went inside, and a good dinner was cooking of all kinds of fish, and a good meal they made of it, and a grand drinking at the end of all kinds of strong spirits. Jack had never felt his head cooler, it must have been the cold water above him; but the old merrow got quite boisterous, and roared out all manner of songs, though Jack couldn't call any of them to mind afterwards. He told Jack his name too — Coomara it was, and Coo to his friends, for by this time they were pretty snug together.

After they'd drunken as much as was comfortable, Coomara took Jack to see his curiosities, and a grand museum of things he'd got, all of them dropped out of the sea. The thing that puzzled Jack most was a great row of wicker baskets, something like lobster pots.

'And what might you keep in those, Coomara?' he said.

'Oh, those are soul cages,' said Coomara.

'But the fish haven't souls, surely,' said Jack.

'No, not they,' said Coomara. 'Those are the souls of fishermen. I like to have them about the place. So whenever there is a big storm up above, I sprinkle those about the sand; and when the souls come down, they are cold and frightened, having just lost their men and they creep in here for warmth; and then it fails them to get out again. And aren't they lucky, now, to have a warm, dry place like this to stay?'

Jack said never a word, but he bent down by the soul cages, and though he could see nothing, he fancied he heard a breath like a sob when old Coo talked of their good luck. So he said goodbye; and old Coo gave him a back up, and shoved him up into the sea; and he shot up faster than he had come down, and threw his cocked hat back as Coomara had told him, and went home very sad to think of the poor souls imprisoned in their lobster cages.

Jack Dogherty turned over and over in his mind how he could free the poor souls, but for a while nothing came to him. He didn't like to ask the Priest, for he didn't want to get Coomara into trouble, and he didn't care to tell his wife or friends, for perhaps a man mightn't be well thought of who had dealings with the merrows; so at last he decided he must ask Coomara to his own house and make him very drunk, and then nip off his cap and go down and free the poor souls so that Coomara would never be the wiser. The first thing was to get his wife out of the way. So Jack turned very pious all of a sudden, and he told his wife it would be a grand thing if she would make a pilgrimage to pray for his soul and the souls of all poor fishermen drowned at sea. His wife was ready enough to go, for whoever heard of a woman would refuse a pilgrimage; and no sooner had he seen her back than Jack nipped over to the merrow's rock and invited old Coomara to come and dine with him at one o'clock next day and to see what he had about the place in the way of drink. Coomara came readily enough; and they kept it up together, drinking and singing; but Jack forgot this time that he had not the sea above him to keep his head cool; and the first thing he knew he wakened up with a black headache, and there was not a sign of old Coomara, who had drunk him under the table and walked off as cool as you please.

Poor Jack was quite downcast to think that the caged souls were as far from their freedom as ever; but luckily Biddy was to be a week away, and before that time was past he had a thought that gave him a glimmer of hope. Coomara was well seasoned to whiskey and brandy and rum; but it was likely he had never tasted a drop of the real Irish potcheen, for that is a spirit that is seldom put upon the sea. Now as it happened, Jack had a keg of it, brewed by his own wife's brother, so he thought he would see what it would do for Coomara. So back he went to the merrow's rock, where he found Coomara very cock-a-hoop at having put him under the table.

'I'll not deny that you're a sturdy drinker, Coomara, said Jack. 'But I have something put aside that you've never tasted, and that's a keg of the real potcheen that I'd kept till last; only you slipped out whilst I was considering to myself for a few moments. Come back tomorrow and you shall have a taste of it; and that's a thing I wouldn't offer to everyone, for it's hard to come by.'

Coomara was very ready to come, for he had a curiosity to taste the stuff; and next day they set to it again. I wouldn't say Jack drank entirely fair, for he put water to what he took and Coomara took it neat, but fair or unfair he drank Coomara under the table; and he was no sooner there than Jack nipped the hat off his head and set off to the rock as fast as he could run. There was nobody to be seen at the bottom of the sea, and that was a lucky thing for Jack, for he'd have been hard put to it to explain what he was doing in Coomara's house. He took a great armful of the soul cages and took them out of the house and turned them up. He saw nothing at all, except it might be a little flicker of light coming out of each of them, and he heard a sound like a faint whistle going past him. He emptied all the soul cages and put them back just as they had been, and then he worked and struggled his way up the roots of the seaweed until he got into the sea again, and so to land. Coomara was still asleep, and when he waked he was so ashamed to be out-drunken that he sneaked off without a word. But he and Jack stayed very good friends, for he never noticed that the soul cages were empty; and often after a storm Jack would make some excuse to go down, and would free all the new souls that had been caught. So they went on in great friendship for many years; until one day Jack threw his stone into the water without success. Coomara never came. Jack did not know what to make of it. Coomara was a young slip of a fellow as merrows went, not more than a couple of hundred years at the most. He couldn't have died on him. So all Jack could think was that Coomara must have flitted and be living in another part of the sea. But Coomara had the second cocked hat, so Jack could never go down to find out.

The Old Man of Cury [1]

An old fisherman of the parish of Cury near the Lizard Point was strolling idly along the beach one day when the tide was low. He raised his eyes and suddenly saw in front of him the prettiest girl he had ever seen in his life. She was sitting on a rock by a deep pool, busily combing her golden hair, which was so long and so thick that it covered her from top to toe. For a few minutes the old man watched her unnoticed; then he said: 'What cheer, young one? And what are you doing there, alone by yourself like?'

The strange girl noticed him for the first time. She looked up with a startled face, and immediately slid over the rock and into the deep pool on the other side. The old man was afraid she might be drowned or hurt, and hurried up the rock to look into the pool. There was the beautiful girl, weeping and shivering; but her gold hair floated on the surface of the water, and through it he could see the movement of a silvery tail. The old man gazed down at her. He had often heard tell of merrymaids, but he had never seen one before. He stood and looked and looked until her sad crying roused his pity.

'Now don't ee take on so, my dear,' he said. 'I'm an old man near my grave, and I wouldn't hurt a hair on that purty head.'

'Oh, what shall I do?' she cried. 'What shall I do?'

'Why, what's the matter then?' he said, so kindly that she told him her troubles.

She and her two children and her husband had swum up when the tide was high into Kynance Cove. Her husband had come out on to the sand to sleep, and the children were playing prettily in the shallow water, so she thought she would explore the strange dry land. She had dragged herself over sand and rocks to look at the sweet-smelling flowers that grew on the short turf; and at length, being weary, she had sat down to comb out her tangled hair. She must have been longer than she thought; for when the fisherman spoke to her she looked up, and saw that the tide was far down and that too wide a strip of sand stretched between her and the sea for her to be able to drag herself over it.

'You're safe enough in this pool,' said the fisherman. 'It's but to wait till the tide's up again, and that won't be so long.'

'But what will happen in the meantime?' said the merrymaid, weeping bitterly. 'My husband will have no dinner; and he is such a brute when he is hungry that he would think nothing of killing and eating the children rather than he would go hungry. Besides he is so jealous that he will think that I have stayed here to talk to a mortal lover. Oh, if only I could get to the sea!'

'Well, if it comes to that, I daresay I could carry ee,' said the fisherman. 'I've not lost all my strength yet, and I daresay you're no great weight.'

'Oh, thank you, thank you!' said the merrymaid. 'If you carry me back to the sea I will give you any three wishes you want.'

So the old fisherman knelt down by the pool, and the merrymaid put her thin, white arms round his neck, and he carried her down to the sea on his back. As they went she told him to wish his three wishes. Any wealth should be his that she could give.

'I don't need gold and silver,' said the fisherman, who was as sensible as he was kind. 'If ee'll give me three things to help the neighbours with I'll be very thankful. Give me the power to break the spells of witchcraft and to heal diseases and to tell where stolen things are hid.'

'You shall have your wishes,' said the merrymaid.

They reached the sea's edge, and the merrymaid put her ivory comb into his hand. 'If you want me, stroke the water three times and I will come,' she said. 'Thank you, my dear old fisherman.' She kissed his cheek and loosened her grasp and slid into the sea.

The fisherman went home with his comb, and he would often go and stroke the sea, so that his friend the merrymaid might come to him. They had long talks together, and sometimes he would take her on his back to where she could watch people walking about on their pretty forked tails, for she had a great curiosity about human ways. He always kept the powers she gave him and put them to good use, and his sons and grandsons had them after him. As for the merry-maid's comb, his descendants keep it proudly to this day.

THE SEAL FISHER AND THE ROANE [1]

NEAR John o' Groats House there was once a fisherman who was the best seal fisher in the North Country. One day when he was out fishing a big dog seal rose near to his boat. He threw his knife at it and struck it; but the seal dived under the water and escaped, and the fisher had to go home without his knife.

As he was sitting down to supper that night there came a knock at the door, and when the fisherman opened it he saw a tall stranger outside, holding two fine horses.

'Are you Peter Ruach, the Seal Fisher?' he asked.

'I am, sir,' said the fisher.

'I have a large order for you for seal skins,' said the stranger. 'If you will come with me I will let you see what you are to do.'

The stranger was so well spoken and the horses so finely harnessed that Peter did not hesitate. He mounted on one horse and the stranger on the other, and they rode through the gathering darkness until they came to the lonely seashore. Presently Peter began to be afraid.

'Stop!' he said. 'Where are you taking me? No one lives along this way.'

'We are nearly there,' said the stranger, and he turned his horse's head towards the edge of the cliff along which they rode.

'Stop!' said Peter in terror.

[1] (Highland.) Keightley, p. 394.

'Sit firmly,' said the stranger, 'and I will bring you safely to my home.'

With that he took the rein of Peter's horse in his hand, and the two horses leapt clean over the towering cliff into the deep, surging sea beneath them. Peter had only time to bend down and cling to his horse's neck before its front hoofs splashed in the water, and it clove the sea like a fish and bore him with it into the depths of the sea. The frightened breath which Peter had taken at the top of the cliff was not all spent when they reached the bottom of the sea, and moved upward into a great cave where the horse stopped.

Peter was astonished to find that he was no longer pressed upon by the water. His clothes were wet by his passage through the sea, but here, at the bottom of the sea, he could breathe fresh air again. He turned to look at his companion and found a seal beside him; but as he looked the seal stripped off its skin and he saw again the stranger who had brought him from his cottage. Several more stately figures came up to him; but they too carried seal skins over their arms. Peter began to understand that he was in the Seal Kingdom. He had often heard it said that the seals only wore their skins for swimming in the water, and could cast them off and appear as men and women; now he really believed it. As he thought of all the seals he had killed and that they must be the brothers and sisters and cousins of the creatures he saw, Peter's courage failed him, and his heart dunted against his side. He remembered that the fairies are said to be revengeful and he was sure that he had been fetched down into the sea to suffer some cruel punishment.

He kept as brave a face as he could, but his companion saw that he was afraid.

'Do not be frightened,' he said. 'Indeed we mean you no harm. Follow me.'

He spoke so kindly that Peter believed him, and found strength to follow him along the winding coral passages of the sea palace. They came at last to a great pillared room, where an old man with a noble face was lying sorely wounded; and, sticking in the wound, Peter saw his own knife.

'This is my father whom you wounded this morning,' said his companion. 'He is our King. Do you wish him to live or to die?'

'Indeed,' said Peter, 'I wish him to live with all my heart. I did not know whom I struck.'

'Then it is in your power to heal him,' said the Seal Prince. 'Draw out the knife, and stroke the wound gently with the flat of it, saying— "All health be with you", and the wound will be healed.'

Peter drew out the knife; and when he had stroked the wound and said the words the flow of blood was staunched, and the King of the Seals raised himself on his elbow as well as he had ever been, while all the Seal People around him shouted for joy.

Peter's seal bent down and kissed his father's hand, and then drew Peter out of the room.

'Come and refresh yourself,' he said. 'I must ask your pardon for the falsehood I used when I came to your house. Nothing would have tempted me to it except the need to save my father's life. Eat and drink and then I will take you to shore again. But we have one thing to ask you — that you will never again throw your knife at a seal. Catch any of the fish of the sea that you like, but leave the seals alone.'

'No need to ask me that,' said Peter, 'after what I have seen today. You had me in your power and I had killed many of your kinsmen, and yet you treated me kindly. May my hand drop off if I ever touch a sealing knife again.'

'That is all we ask,' said the Seal Prince. 'Come with me to the banquet.'

Many men would have been afraid to touch fairy food; but Peter trusted the Seal People, and sat down to the banquet with them. The more he saw of them the better he liked them, there was such nobility in their merriment, and not one of all the crowd reproached him with the slaughter he had done among them in past years.

When the banquet was over the Seal Prince called for their horses and led Peter by another way home and to his cottage door. Here he gave him a large, green bag.

'You will be the poorer,' he said, 'for the loss of our skins; but if ever you need money take a gold coin out of this bag. It will be long before you get to the bottom of it.'

With this he gathered up the loose rein of Peter's horse and rode quickly away. Peter carried the green bag with him into his cottage. He used it sparingly, and it never failed in his lifetime. Nor did his friendship with the seals fail either; for he would often go out to the rocks when the tide was low and talk with the

Seal People who came up from the depths to meet him. He knew more than any man of the secrets of the sea. And so he lived happily all his days.

PARALLEL STORIES: There are several other stories in which the seals are given this character. Perhaps the closest is the Shetland story of 'Ollavatinus and his Mother Gioga'.

THE WATER HORSE AND THE WATER BULL[1]

THE Highland Water Bulls are not dangerous to man like the Water Horses. They are black, shaggy and large, and it is a great enriching of any common stock of cattle to get a water bull among them. They may chiefly be recognized by their ears, which are more human in shape than the ears of ordinary cattle.

There was once, in one of the islands near Islay, a rich farmer with a great stock of cattle. One year one of the cows gave birth to a little calf which was different from all the other calves. An old, knowledgeable woman who lived on the farm looked at it long and said: 'This is no common calf; it is the son of a water bull. Keep it lodged by itself, and feed it for seven years upon the milk of three cows and you will not see its equal in the country.'

This was done, and the calf grew into a great bull, black and shaggy and wild, but without its equal for strength and beauty.

The farmer had one daughter, a beautiful girl with long black hair and soft brown eyes, who loved to wander alone by the shores of the little salt loch. One day on the shore she met a young man, dark and tall and handsome, a stranger to her. They walked along together and talked, and he looked at her with dark, burning eyes that had great power over her. At last they sat down together, and he laid his head on her knee

---

[1] Campbell, *Tales of the Western Highlands.*

and asked her to comb out his hair. The girl began on his dark, tangled locks, laughing and talking as she worked. But suddenly her talk and laughter stopped. There among the dark hair, growing on the head as it grows on a stone under the water, was a tangle of the green shining water weed that grows in salt lochs.

'Heaven preserve us!' thought the girl. 'What creature is this I have under my hands? It must be the dreadful sea horse that can take human shape. It's best for me to be out of this.'

But she was a brave girl with a steady mind, and she knew that if she started up, or gave so much as a gasp it would cost her her life. So she combed on smoothly, and presently when her voice was steady she began to sing a lullaby. The dreadful head on her lap lay more heavily and the eyes of the stranger closed. Soon he began to breathe evenly. The girl put her hands behind her and untied her apron. Then, inch by inch, still singing smoothly, she edged her knees away from the stranger's head, until she could lay it, still on her apron, softly on the mound of turf where she had been sitting. Then she slipped away and ran like the wind towards her father's house. She had nearly reached it when she heard a thundering of hoofs behind her, and saw a wild, shaggy grey horse, with bared teeth and dark fiery eyes, hot on her heels. She shrieked out in her despair, for she knew he would be on her long before she could reach the farm. But help was near. The old woman was standing at the yard gate, and when she heard the girl shriek she hobbled to the shed where the water bull was kept and opened the door. The great bull came slowly out, looking about it.

Then it saw the girl running and the water horse hard behind, and it lowered its head and bellowed, and charged straight at the horse. The two met, tossing and goring and biting and kicking so that the turf flew around them, and the noise was frightful. But

step by step the brave bull drove the water horse backward until they reached the loch. They plunged in, still fighting, above and below the water, until they were out into the deep parts of it and vanished.

Two days later the bull's body, all torn about, was washed up to the shore, but not a sign nor a bit of the water horse was ever seen. Neither strange man nor strange horse ever appeared by the lochside again.

PARALLEL STORIES: Stories very like this are told about the Water Horse and the Kelpie all over the Highlands. Campbell tells another story about the Water Bull in which the bull is freed from a charm by the help he has given.

THE GWRAIG AND THE THREE BLOWS [1]

A GOOD number of the Welsh fairies were water fairies, and there are many stories of these Ladies of the Lake, or Gwraigs, as they are called in Wales. Here is one of the completest of them.

There was once a young farmer who had often heard of a gwraig on the lake near. She was a most beautiful maiden, with a pale face and flowing golden hair, and she rowed a golden boat about the lake with a golden oar. He heard so much about her that he grew curious to see her; and one New Year's Eve he went down to the water side, for that is one of the likeliest times for seeing spirits. As the moon rose she was there, and he thought her even lovelier than report had made her. All night long he stood by the edge of the lake watching her, silent and entranced; but when dawn came she began to fade away, and then he cried out with a strong voice, begging her to come home with him and be his bride. She answered only by a faint moan, and vanished away. The farmer returned home a different man. He could neither eat nor sleep for the beauty of the gwraig. Every night he went to the lake, but he saw nothing, or only a far-away rippling in the wake of her boat, or the faint flash of her golden oar. At length in despair he went to a wise man and asked him what he could do to win the gwraig. The wise man thought the wooing would be hard, but not impossible, and advised the farmer to woo her with gifts of bread and cheese.

[1] Sikes, p. 40.

Beginning at Midsummer the farmer dropped bread and cheese every night into the lake, and so continued until New Year's Eve. This was the time at which he most hoped for success. He dressed himself in his best and took with him seven white loaves and a great cheese. He threw in the loaves one by one and the cheese after them. The cheese had hardly disappeared under the water when he saw a movement in a distant part of the lake, and the golden boat came speeding towards him. The farmer fell on his knees, and the gwraig stepped out on to land. He begged her to marry him, and she consented; but she warned him that if he struck her three times, however lightly, she must leave him.

She brought with her a great dowry of water cattle, which are finer than any bred on land, and they went to his farm together. Time did not diminish their love for each other. Her beauty seemed to him brighter every day, and she was a tender and devoted wife. But she had queer ways of thinking, and of behaving too at times. He would not have minded it when they were by themselves, but he wished she would behave more like other people before the neighbours.

One day, for instance, when they had been four years married, they went together to a christening. Everyone was merry except the farmer's wife, who suddenly burst into tears in the middle of the party.

'What's the matter? Are you ill?' said her husband.

'No, no,' she said. 'But how can I help weeping when I think of this poor child, born into a world of sorrow and sin and pain?'

'Be quiet,' said her husband. 'Why can't you behave

like other people?' And he gave her an impatient push.

She turned to him with the tears wet on her lashes.

'Be careful, my dear,' she said to him in a low tone. 'That is once you have struck me.'

Not many months later the baby died, and the farmer and his wife went to the funeral. If the gwraig had been sad among merrymakers before she was now merry among mourners. Suddenly in the midst of the weeping she burst out into a peal of laughter, and began to sing and dance.

'Are you mad?' said her husband angrily.

'How can you all weep?' she said. 'The dear babe has been snatched away from pain and sin, and is gone to be good and happy for ever. How can we help rejoicing?'

But her husband tapped her impatiently, and she looked at him with sudden sorrow.

'My dear,' she said, 'that is the second time. Be very careful, for you have only one more chance.'

Some time later the farmer and his wife went to a neighbour's wedding — an old man who had married a young and pretty wife. Amongst all the laughter and joking the gwraig sat silent, and her husband began to be afraid of what she might do. Suddenly she burst into tears and started up, wringing her hands.

'Oh, take me away!' she said. 'How can I bear it! Take me away! This is the devil's work, when youth is wedded to old age, not for love or pity but for the sake of gold. Oh, there can be no blessing on this match!'

The bridegroom rose offended, the neighbours sat all eyes, the bride began to weep. The farmer, angered and in consternation, struck at his wife, crying: 'Hold your tongue!'

She rose at once. 'The third blow is struck, my dearest,' she said. 'Goodbye.'

She kissed him, and slipped out of his arms. He ran out after her; but he only reached his home in time to see the last of her cattle disappear under the water of the lake.

PARALLEL STORIES: Sikes gives two other stories very like this. In one the prohibition is that the Fairy Wife may not be touched with cold iron, and the blow is purely accidental. It has a close resemblance, too, to 'Wild Edric', as well as to the many stories of 'Swan Maidens' and 'Seal Wives'. Campbell's story of 'Diarmid and the Daughter of the King of the Under-waves' has something the same plot.

THE BROWN MAN OF THE MUIRS [1]

ABOUT two hundred years ago two young men went out hunting on Elsdon Moor, near Newcastle. They had good sport, and in the middle of the day they sat down to eat, and the younger one wandered down to a little stream to drink. As he was kneeling by the water he heard a harsh voice, and, looking up, he saw the strangest creature he had ever seen. It was the Brown Man of the Muirs. He was small, but square and strong, dressed in clothes like withered bracken, with red, frizzled hair on his head, and great, rolling eyes like an angry bull's.

'How dare ye come here, ye callant?' he said. 'Killing the birds and beasts that are in my charge. Gin nits and blaeberries dae for me that am their King sud they nae no gude enough for ye? Come owre here, and I'll show ye the denner I get.'

The young man was daunted for a minute, but he was the wildest lad in the countryside, and he stood up and put his foot on a tussock to jump. Just then his friend cried behind him: 'Willie, Willie! Whaur are ye?'

He looked round, and that instant the Brown Man vanished.

'Did ye see the secht I saw?' he said.

'What secht?' said his friend.

Willie told what he had seen and heard, and suggested that they should cross and look for the Brown Man.

[1] Henderson.

'Heaven forfend ye should cross that burn!' said his friend. 'It was nocht but the running water saved ye. He would hae torn ye limb from limb if ye had crossed. Come hame; we'll hunt nae mair the day.'

Willie was enough daunted to be ready to leave his sport; but as they went back a brace of grouse sprang up with a great whirring under their feet, and without a thought Willie raised his fowling piece and shot.

As the bird fell a pang went through him. He shivered, and went shivering home. He never throve after, and in a short time he died, for the Brown Man of the Muirs had laid his curse on him.

PART FOUR

MONSTERS, WITCHES AND GIANTS

MONSTERS, WITCHES AND
GIANTS

THE Monsters of fairyland are of many shapes,
and most of them can take any shape at will. A
good many of them have already been mentioned.
Some are water spirits, like Nuckelavee and Shellycoat
and the Kelpie, some, like Pooka, are close relations
of the Hobgoblins, but a few are left over who are,
some demons and ghosts in animal form, and some
their unexplained and inexplicable selves.

The Bogie Beast is the best known of these, who
can take any form he pleases, and the Picktree Brag
is like him, though its normal shape is that of a great
longlegged colt, with fiery eyes. Almost the same are
the Brash and Padfoot, both named from the noise

they make as they move along beside the benighted traveller. Church Grim, who haunts many Yorkshire churchyards, is probably the spirit of the animal sacrificed there to propitiate the spirits of the underworld; the Black Dog is sometimes a ghost but more often a demon, alarming, but only really dangerous if spoken to or touched; the Dandy Dogs and the Wish Hounds are demons.

A few, beautiful in form, are monsters only in iniquity. Such are the Baobhan Sith, beautiful young women with the feet of goats, who meet young men in lonely places, dance with them and suck their blood. Besides the beasts there were the monsters of the dragon kind, the Lambton Worm, Meister Stoorworm and the like. Often these loathsome forms were the result of an enchantment, but many were authentic dragons. A large number, though not all, of these were sea monsters.

Most of the witches of folk lore were only old women who had sold themselves to the devil and not fairies at all; but a few, like Cailleach Bheur and Milton's Blue Meagre Hag were of true fairy nature. These were very near to the wizard giants of the type of that in 'Nix Nought Nothing' and that in the 'Battle of the Birds'. The stone-moving witch of my story I take to be more related to the Fomorians than to the usual old women turned hares of the stories, though the distinction is a delicate one. There are two types of giants, the wizard type, who are probably large and small at will since their daughters seem to be of normal size, and the large, stupid giants whom it was Jack's duty to outwit. Both are generally cannibals.

Here is a list of the Monsters who will be found in the Dictionary at the end.

Afanc, Aughisky, Baobhan Sith, Bargest, Black Annis, Black Dogs, Bodach, Boobrie, Brollachan, Bug-a-Boo, Cait Sith, Capelthwaite, Ca Sith, Caval Usteg, Church Grim, Cwn Annwn, The Devil's Dandy Dogs, Dunnie, Dunters, Fideal, Fomorians, Fuath, Gabriel Hounds, Gally-Trot, Gentle Annie, Grant, Grindylow, Hedley Kow, Hobyahs, Kelpie, Llamhigyn y Dwr, Mauthe Doog, Muileartach, Neagle, Nuckelavee, Padfoot, Picktree Brag, Rawhead-and-Bloody-Bones, Redcap, Shag, Shock, Shriker, Shoopiltee, Tangie, Tanterabogus, Thrumpin, Tom Dockin, Tom Poker, Wisht Hounds, Wryneck.

STORIES

BILLY B——'S ADVENTURE [1]

YOU see, sir, as how I'd been a clock dressing at
Gurston (Grassington), and I'd staid rather lat,
and maybe getten a lile sup o' spirit; but I war
far from being drunk, and knowed everything that
passed. It war about eleven o'clock when I left, and
it war at back end o' t' year, and a most admirable
neet it war. The moon war verra breet, and I nivver
seed Kylstone Fell plainer in a' my life. Now, you see,
sir, I war passing down t' Mill loine, and I heerd
summat come past me — brush, brush, brush, wi'
chains rattlin' a' the while, but I seed nothing; and I
thought to myself, now this is a most mortal queer
thing. And I then stuid still and luiked about me;
but I seed nothing at aw, nobbut the two stane wa's
on each side o' t'mill loine. Then I heard again this
brush, brush, brush, wi' the chains; for you see, sir,
when I stood still it stopped, and then, thowt I, this
mun be a Bargest, that sae much is said about; and I
hurried on toward t' wood brig; for they say as how
this Bargest cannot cross a watter; but, Lord, sir,
when I gat o'er t' brig, I heerd this same again; so it
mun either have crossed t' watter or have gone round
by the spring heed! And then I became a valiant man,
for I were a bit freekened afore; and, thinks I, I'll turn
and hev a peep at this thing; so I went up Greet Bank

---

[1] (Northumberland.) Hone, *Everyday Book*.

towards Linton, and heerd this brush, brush, brush, wi' the chains aw the way, but I seed nothing; then it ceased all of a sudden. So I turned back to go hame; but I'd hardly reached the door when I heerd again this brush, brush, brush, and the chains going down

towards t' Holin House; and I followed it, and the moon there shone verra breet, and I seed its tail! Then thowt I, thou owd thing, I can say I'se seen thee now: so I'll away hame.

When I gat to the door there were a grit thing like a sheep, but it war larger, ligging across the threshold o' t' door, and it war woolly like; and I says, 'Git up!' and it wouldn't git up. Then says I, 'Stir thysel!' and it wouldn't stir itself. And I grew valiant, and I raised t' stick to baste it wi'; and then it luiked at me, and

173

sich oies, they did glower, and war as big as saucers and like a cruelled ball. First there war a red ring, then a blue one, then a white one; and these rings grew less and less till they cam to a dot! Now I war none feared on it, tho it grin'd at me fearfully, and I kept on saying, 'Git up', and 'Stir thysel', and the wife heerd as how I war at t' door, and she cam to oppen it; and then this thing gat up and walked off, for it war mare freeten'd o' t'owd wife than it war o' me; and I told the wife, and she said as how it war Bargest; but I never seed it since — and that's a true story.

CLACH MOR AND THE WITCH OF BADENOCH[1]

At the bottom of Glen Fernate, near the Kirkmichael road on the way to Balmoral is a great stone known as Clach Mor. This is its story.

The Great Comyn of Badenoch had planned to build himself a magnificent castle. It was to be too big for a common builder, so he asked the help of one of the witches of Badenoch. She promised to carry the stones for it in her apron up to Badenoch; but she could not find anywhere in Scotland two stones big enough to make the doorposts. At last a witch from Man told her of two great stones which would just suit her. She flew over to Man, gathered up one of the stones in her apron, and set off for Badenoch, flying low because of the weight of it. It was a clear, moonlight night, and as she flew up Glen Fernate the huntsman had come back from setting his snares, and he looked up and saw a great mass above him in the sky.

'God preserve us!' he cried, and at the Holy Name the witch's apron strings broke, and a great mass came tumbling down just beside him. And there it lies to this day, a great block twenty feet high and seventy round, and weighing something like a thousand tons. As for the witch, it failed her to get an apron string as strong again, and the Great Comyn's great castle is unbuilt to this day.

[1] A local legend of Perthshire.

The Old Woman and the Hedley Kow [1]

THERE was once an old woman who was very poor. By running errands for the neighbours she could just manage to scrape together enough to live; but she had a merry heart, and however hard her life might be she always felt herself to be lucky.

One evening as dusk was coming she was trotting home after a hard day's work, when in a lonely part of the road she saw an old pot lying.

'Who'd leave a thing like that there?' she said. 'Maybe it's got a hole in it; but even if it has it will come in useful to me, for I can put a plant in it and set it in my window.' And she stooped down to lift up the pot. It had no hole in it at all, and it was full of gold pieces.

'Lawk a mercy!' said the old woman, and she looked all around to see who might be the owner of a pot like that; but there was no one in sight, and she began to think that findings are keepings. She tried to lift it, but it was too heavy for her, so she tied the corner of her shawl to it and began to drag it along the road.

'Well!' she thought to herself, 'I've often thought I was lucky and this proves it. A whole potful of gold! Why, how rich and great I shall be! Now, I wonder what I'll do with it? I might buy myself a new teapot and a feather bed and a padded petticoat and a pig, and a cow, I daresay, too. Or I might dig a hole and bury it in the garden, and just keep a piece with a hole in it to turn over in my hands.'

[1] Jacobs, *More English Fairy Tales*, p. 50.

And so she trotted on till she was quite out of breath, and turned to have another look at the pot. It was no pot at all, but only a great piece of silver tied into a corner of her shawl.

She stared and stared and rubbed her eyes.

'Well, now, I could have sworn it was an iron pot, full of gold pieces, and here it is a bar of shining silver. That will do better than gold, much better; for the gold would have been a trouble and a worry to me, and have made me grander than my neighbours. No, the silver's much better. I shall be rich with the silver, and I'd have got careful and griping on the gold.'

And so she went on, thinking how she could sell the silver and what she would buy with the money, until her breath was quite gone again, and she stopped to look at her bundle. The bar of silver was gone from the corner of her shawl, and in its place was a great piece of old iron. The old woman was amazed.

'My head must be leaving me!' she said. 'Here was I quite certain it was silver, and all the time it was old iron. Well, but that's much better than the silver. It would have puzzled me to sell a great piece of silver like that. People would have asked questions. But I could sell the iron for good pennies. Pennies are happier than silver any day; they come and go lighter. Yes, yes, I'm lucky and no mistake to have found a good piece of old iron like that.'

She was so cheered by the thought that she hurried briskly on, and got her load to the cottage door as if it was no heavier than air. Then, when she'd opened her door, she turned to lift the iron into the house. There was no iron there, only a great big round stone, tied up in her shawl. For a moment the old woman was quite taken aback; then she said:

'A stone it is! A stone the whole time. Well, isn't it fortunate I didn't know it, because I shouldn't have carried it all that long way, and yet a stone is the very thing I most want at this moment to keep my gate shut, so that the pigs and the poultry don't get in. A stone will be better than gold to me, because it will save my seeds and vegetables from getting trampled and eaten.'

And she bent down to roll the stone into place.

There it lay a smooth hard stone; but as she touched it it grew soft and warm. She started back and it shot up on four long, thin legs. Then it gave a whicker, and it lashed a long, hairy tail, and away it went, curvetting and capering and whinneying to think of the trick it had played on the old woman.

But if it laughed the old woman laughed too.

'The Hedley Kow!' said she. 'The Hedley Kow! Why, I've heard of it from my old Grannie, but the Parson himself hasn't seen it, and to think of me hauling it up and down, and rolling it here and rolling it there as if it had been a stray kitten. Lucky! Why, if I'd been the Queen of Sheba I couldn't have acted grander.'

And if she had been the Queen of the Kingdoms of the World she could not have felt happier.

PARALLEL STORIES: 'Mr. Vinegar', Grimm's 'Hans in Luck', and Hans Andersen's 'The Goodman is always Right' are like this in the continued changes for the worse, but they have no supernatural element.

THE LAMBTON WORM[1]

MANY hundreds of years ago there was an Heir of
Lambton who was a wild and godless young man.
One Sunday morning when everyone else was getting
ready to go to church he went out to fish in the river
Wear. He fished patiently for some time, but with as
little success as he deserved, and when the tenants and
servants passed on the way to church they heard him
cursing and swearing to himself because he had caught
nothing. They looked at each other and shook their
heads and hurried on, for they felt that something ill
would follow such conduct. Sure enough they had
hardly gone before the Heir's rod bent suddenly, and
he knew that he had hooked a great fish. He had hard
work playing it, and no sooner had he got it on land
than it spat out the hook, and lay, jerking and
wriggling among the stones, a great, dark, ugly,
lizardlike thing. The Heir did not like the look of it,
and he flung it into a well near the river, which is
called the Worm's Well to this day. Just as he did so
a venerable-looking stranger passed, hurrying along to
church, for the bells were just stopping. But he paused
for a moment to ask the Heir what sport he had had.

'I've been fishing,' said the Heir, 'and I do believe
I've caught the Devil himself, for I've never seen the
like. Go to the well and have a look at him.'

The stranger peered in.

'It's a queer thing,' he said. 'It's like a great eft,

1 Henderson, p. 287.

179

but it has nine holes round its mouth. If you ask me it bodes no good.'

He went on; and the Heir gathered his tackle and went home, for he had no more heart for fishing.

The stranger was right — the queer fish boded no good. It lay in the well quiet enough for a while; but it grew and grew and grew. The Heir of Lambton was a soberer man since the day he caught it; and after a few years he went away to the Crusades to make atonement for his wild ways. While he was away the worm climbed out of the well and began to lay waste the countryside. It was still like an eft, with four legs and great scaly tail, but it stood higher than a man from foot to shoulder, and its tail was so long that it could curl itself three times round the Worme Hill, where you can still see the marks its great weight made as it lay wound round, watching the countryside. At length it cleared the countryside of sheep and cattle, and came lurching along towards Lambton Hall. The old Lord, the servants, and the ruined and plundered people from miles round were gathered there with the stock they had been able to save, and they debated anxiously what they could do. There was no time to be lost, and the old steward suggested that they should fill the great stone trough outside the Hall with milk to stay the beast's appetite. It took the milk of nine cows to fill it, but the worm was satisfied with the drink, and went back to Worme Hill for the night.

Every day, night and morning, the worm came over to the hall for its drink, and to some extent this seemed to satisfy it; but the countryside was growing poorer

and poorer. At length the Heir came home, and saw
what harm he had done. He went to look at the worm,
coiled round Worme Hill, and determined to fight it.
But when he told his father what he meant to do his
father begged him to think no more of such a thing.
Many knights had set out to kill the worm before this
and had died in the attempt. It was not only that the
worm was great and fierce, with long, strangling coils
and bony jaws, but the most fearful thing about it was
its power of joining together when it was cut, so that
the best swordsman might as well cut the air as sever
its limbs.

'You are safe home again at last, my son,' said his
father, 'a good sober man and a brave fighter; let me
have the joy of your company in my few last years.'

The Heir listened to his father, but he felt more and
more that the evil which he had brought upon the
country must be for him to lift; so at length he went to
the Wise Woman of Lambton and asked her how he
could destroy the worm. He listened first patiently to
her reproaches, and he had many to hear, but at last
she told him what he must do.

He must carry his strongest armour to the smith
and have it studded with long, sharp spikes. He must
take his stand in the middle of the river and attack
the worm as it went across to its evening meal. If he
did this he might have some chance of success. But
because it was he who had brought this curse on the
country a further penance was asked of him. Before
he went to the fight he must vow that he would kill
the first living thing that came to meet him on his
return. If he broke his vow she warned him that for

nine generations not one of his heirs should die in his bed. He thanked her, took the vow in Brugeford Chapel, and went home to get ready for the fight.

Three days later, just before sunset, the Heir stood in his steel-studded armour on a shoal of rock in the middle of the Wear and waited for the enemy to pass. The river was high, and the water foamed past him, which answered his hopes. As the sun sank the great worm uncoiled itself from the hill opposite and came lurching down towards the stream. As it passed near his rock the Heir struck out at it. It turned quickly and fiercely on him and wrapped him in its coils. The good plate armour stood the first shock, and the spikes pierced the worm's scaly skin. The more furiously it hugged the more it wounded itself; until the Heir got his sword arm free and lopped off a leg. It had no chance to join again, for the swift stream carried the limb away. And so, by stroke after stroke,

the Heir conquered his enemy, and weak and wearied and in the darkness he made his way back to land, and blew feebly on the horn that was to be the sign of his victory. It was the sign too to let loose the favourite dog which, with a heavy heart, the Heir had decided to

sacrifice. But through these hours of the fight his
father had been waiting in dreadful suspense, and as
the darkness fell he became sure that his son was killed
like the other knights. In the middle of his grief he
suddenly heard a faint and breathless blast upon the
horn. He never paused to think, but ran out to see if
his son was really safe.

The Heir dropped the point of his reddened sword
as he saw him. He could not touch his father. In his
perplexity he blew a stronger blast, and the servants
heard him this time, and loosed the dog. It bounded
towards its master, and he laid it dead before either
knew what had happened. But it was too late to lift
the curse. His father had reached him before the dog;
and for nine generations no lord of Lambton died in
his bed.

THE ORIGIN OF THE WREKIN [1]

A GOOD many years before any of us were born it happened that the Mayor of Shrewsbury had given mortal offence to a Welsh giant. The giant considered how best he could avenge himself, and decided that he would bury Shrewsbury with the mayor inside. So he dug up a good spadeful of earth and set out on his way. Anyone who has carried a spadeful of earth across a garden will know that it is a tedious job, and very soon the giant began to consider how far it was to Shrewsbury. As he looked about him he saw a little ribbon of white road at his feet, and, very tiny on it a cobbler's apprentice, who was coming back from Shrewsbury with a bundle of shoes that he had collected to mend slung over his back.

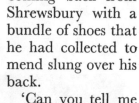

'Can you tell me where Shrewsbury is, my little fellow'? said the giant, roaring down from the heavens. The cobbler turned back his head and piped up into the sky:

[1] (A Shropshire Legend.) Miss C. S. Burne, *Shropshire Folk-Lore*, p. 2.

'What do you want with Shrewsbury, mighty sir?'

'Why,' said the giant, 'you must know the Mayor of Shrewsbury has insulted me something cruel, he has indeed, and I am bringing this spadeful of earth to cover him and all his town too.'

The great mass of earth towered like a floating mountain in the sky above the cobbler, and he saw that if anyone was to save Shrewsbury it must be he.

'Dear me, sir,' he said very simply. 'You've a terrible long tramp ahead of you. I'm from Shrewsbury myself, and only look at all the pairs of shoes I've worn out on the way.'

'You don't say so!' said the giant. 'I thought it was quite near. Dear me! I'll never carry this great spadeful all that way. I'd best go home.'

With that he emptied his spadeful, and there it stands to this day as the Wrekin, then he scraped his boots with his spade, and left High Ercall Point behind him, and then he went back to Wales. And that is how a brave cobbler saved Shrewsbury at the risk of his life; for he was as nearly as possible buried under the Wrekin when the giant put down his spadeful.

A DICTIONARY OF FAIRIES

A DICTIONARY OF FAIRIES

THE AFANC (Welsh. Rhys). A Welsh water demon who haunted a pool in the river Conway, and dragged down all living things into its depths. He was at length captured through the treachery of a girl whom he loved, and dragged ashore by oxen. The Deluge, in Welsh folklore, is connected with a monstrous crocodile called Afanc i Llyn.

AINSEL (Northumbrian). The name of the little fairy girl in the story of Ainsel quoted by Keightley.

AUGHISKY (Irish). An Irish form of Water Kelpy who preys on cattle.

AWD GOGGIE (Yorkshire. *County Folk-Lore*. East Riding). A demon who guards unripe fruit in the orchards.

THE BANSHEE The Banshee is known both in Ireland and Scotland. In Scotland she is sometimes called The Little Washer of Sorrow, or the Washer at the Ford. She can be heard wailing by the river side as she washes the clothes of the man destined for death. If a mortal can seize and hold her, she must tell the name of the doomed man, and also grant three wishes. She is no beauty, for she has only one nostril, a large, starting-out front tooth, and web feet. The Irish banshee only wails for the members of the old families. When several banshees wail in chorus, it foretells the death of someone very great or holy. The banshee has long streaming hair and a grey cloak over a green dress. Her eyes are fiery red from continual weeping.

In the Highlands of Scotland the word 'banshi' means only a fairy woman, and is chiefly used for the fairies who marry mortals.

THE BAOBAN SITH (Highland). Malignant, blood-sucking spirits, who sometimes appeared as hoodie crows or ravens, but generally as beautiful girls, with long, trailing green dresses hiding their deer's hooves.

There is a story of four young men who sheltered by night in a deserted shieling, where they were joined by four beautiful girls who offered themselves as partners. The one of the four who was making mouth music suddenly noticed drops of blood falling from his companions. In a panic he escaped, pursued by his partner; but he took refuge among the horses, and she could not touch him. In the morning when he returned, he found the bloodless bodies of his companions. Their partners had been the terrible Baobhan Sith.

THE BARGEST (Yorkshire). A creature of something the same kind as the Bogie Beast. It sometimes appears in human form, but generally as an animal. In the fishing villages, a bargest funeral is a presage of death. The bargest in whatever form has eyes like burning coals; it has generally claws, horns and a tail, and is girdled with a clanking chain.

BENDITH Y MAMAU 'The Mother's Blessing' is the Glamorganshire name for the fairies. Amongst the usual fairy characteristics, they elf-ride horses, leaving them broken-winded. They visit houses and bowls of milk are left out for them.

BILLY BLIND A friendly domestic spirit of the Border Country, chiefly mentioned in ballads. He wears a bandage over his eyes. Auld Hoodie and Robin Hood are perhaps only different names for the same spirit. Billy Blind's chief function seems to be to give good advice. It was he who advised and helped Burd Isobel in the 'Ballad of Young Bekie', and it was the Billy Blind whose advice cured the young wife bewitched by her mother-in-law.

BLACK ANNIS (Leicestershire). A malignant hag with a blue face and only one eye, very like the Highland Cailleach Bheur in character. Her cave was in the Dane Hills, but has been filled up. She devoured lambs and young children.

BLACK DOGS The Black Dog is large — about the size of a young calf — black and shaggy, with fiery eyes. It does no harm if left alone; but anyone who speaks to it or touches it is struck senseless, and dies soon after. There are stories of the Black Dog from all over the country. One haunted the guard room of Peel Castle in Man. There are stories about it in Buckinghamshire, Hertford, Cambridge, Suffolk, Lancashire, Dorset and Devon. There is a very good and full account of Black Dogs in *English Fairy and Folk Tales*.

BLACK STOCKINGS A mischievous spirit in black stockings and velvet hose which used to stop horses on Asthall hill in Oxfordshire. There is an old burial mound near.

THE BLUE MEN OF THE MINCH (Highland. See Mackenzie's *Scottish Folk-Lore and Folk Life*). These Blue Men belong entirely to the Minch, and particularly haunt the strait between Long Island and the Shiant Islands. They are a malignant kind of mermen, but they are blue all over. They come swimming out to seize and wreck ships that enter the strait; but a ready tongue, and particularly a facility in rhyming, will baffle them. They have no power over the captain who can answer them quickly and keep the last word. Beyond their activities as wreckers they conjure up storms by their restlessness. The weather is only fine when the Blue Men are asleep. The Islanders think they are fallen angels like the fairies and the Merry Dancers, as the Aurora Borealis is called there.

BOCAN OR BAUCHAN A Highland spirit, something between a hobgoblin and a boggart. Campbell gives a story of one who alternately helped and tried to harm his master. He was so constant that he followed him when he emigrated to Australia, and helped to clear his fields there.

BODACHAN SABHAILL (Highland. The Little Old Man of the Barn). A barn brownie, who takes pity on old men, and threshes the corn and binds the straw for them.

BOOMAN (Shetland and Orkney). A brownie-like hobgoblin. His name is preserved elsewhere in the singing game of 'Booman is dead and gone', found in Lady Gomme. In Yorkshire boh-man is another name for the bargest.

BODACH The Scottish form of bugbear or bug-a-boo. He comes down the chimney to fetch naughty children.

BOGGART A north country spirit. He is like a mischievous type of brownie. He is exactly the same as the poltergeist in his activities and habits.

BOGLE The Scottish version of the Yorkshire boggart, though perhaps less exclusively domestic in his habits.

THE BOOBRIE (Highland). A gigantic water bird which inhabits the Lochs of Argyllshire. It has a loud, harsh voice and webbed feet, and it gobbles up sheep and cattle. It is something like a great cormorant in shape.

BONELESS Mentioned by Reginald Scot in his *Discoverie of Witchcraft*, but he gives no particulars about it.

THE BROLLACHAN Brollachan is the Gaelic for a shapeless thing, and it is probably something like Reginald Scot's 'Boneless'. There is the story of one, the child of a fuath, told by Campbell. It is something the same plot as Ainsel.

BROTHER MIKE A little fairy in a Suffolk folk tale much like Skillywidden.

THE BROWNIE The best known of the industrious domestic hobgoblins. The brownie's land is over all the North of England and up into the Highlands of Scotland. The brownie is small, ragged and shaggy. Some say he has a nose so small as to be hardly more than two nostrils. He is willing to do all odd jobs about a house, but sometimes he untidies what has been left tidy. There are several stories of brownies riding to fetch the nurse for their mistress. The brownie can accept no payment, and the surest way to drive it away is to leave it a suit of clothes. Bread and milk and other dainties can be left unobtrusively, but even they must not be openly offered. The Cornish browney is of the same nature. His special office is to get the bees to settle. When the bees swarm the housewife beats a tin, and calls out: 'Browney! Browney!' until the browney comes invisibly to take charge.

THE BROWN MAN OF THE MUIRS (Border Country). A spirit of the moors, who guards the wild life, but is malignant and dangerous to man.

BUCCAS OR KNOCKERS (Cornish). These are the spirits of the mines, something like the German kobolds. They are said to be the spirits of the Jews who once worked the tin mines, and who are not allowed to rest because of their wicked practices. They are, however, friendly to the miners, and knock to warn them of disaster, and also to show what seams are likely to be profitable.

BUG-A-BOO, BUGBEAR, BOGGLE-BO There are a great variety of names for this bogie, which is generally used to frighten children into good behaviour.

BULL-BEGGAR Mentioned by Reginald Scot. He is one of the spirits for whom milk is put out. Keightley suggests that bull-beggar may be a corruption of bug-bear.

THE BUGAN A form of bogie from Cheshire and Shropshire.

THE BWBACHOD The Welsh brownie people. They are friendly and industrious, but they dislike

195

dissenters and teetotallers. Sikes gives an amusing story of a Bwbach and his quarrel with a Methodist Minister.

Bwca   The Welsh boggart.

The Bwganod   The Welsh bogies.

Cailleach Bheur   (Highland. The Blue Hag). A giant hag who seems to typify winter, for she goes about smiting the earth with her staff so that it grows hard. When spring comes and she is conquered, she flings her staff in disgust into a whin bush or under a holly tree, where grass never grows. She is the patroness of deer and wild boars. Many hills are associated with her, particularly Ben Nevis and Schiehallion. Her general appearance is terrible and hideous, but in some stories she changes at times into a most beautiful maiden. There is a version of the 'Wife of Bath's Tale' told of her, and she is also the villainess of a story rather like 'Nix Nought Nothing'. At times she also turns into a sea-serpent. Particulars of her are given in Mac-kenzie's *Scottish Folk-Lore and Folk Life* and she is mentioned in Campbell.

Cait Sith   (Highland. The Fairy Cat). A large black cat with a white spot on the breast which belongs to the fairies. Perhaps the story of 'The King of the Cats' is about one of these Cait Sith, though it has been anglicized.

196

THE CAPELTHWAITE (North Country). A spirit like the Black Dog, who had, however, the power of appearing in the form of any quadruped. · One haunted Capelthwaite barn, near Milnethorpe. He herded cattle and performed other kindnesses for the farm people, but he was not lucky to meet abroad. Drunken men particularly suffered from his attacks.

CA SITH (Highland. The Fairy Dog). This is a great dog, as large as a bullock and with a dark green coat. He is very like the English Black Dog.

THE CAULD LAD OF HILTON A brownie haunting Hilton Castle who is definitely described as a ghost, and yet was laid, as brownies are always laid, by the present of a cloak and hood.

CAVAL USTEG The Manx water horse.

CHURCH GRIM (Yorkshire). A creature which haunts the church by night, and never stirs from it except in very dark, stormy weather. It used to toll the bell at midnight, and the clergyman reading the funeral service would sometimes catch a glimpse of it sitting at the church tower window, and could tell from its looks whether the buried man was saved or lost.

CHURN-MILK PEG (West Yorkshire). A wood spirit who protects unripe nuts from children. She smokes a pipe.

CLURICAN An Irish fairy, nearly allied to a leprechaun, though Keightley gives a story of one who
is very near to the ordinary hobgoblin type. His
name was Wildbear, and he kept the cellar of
a Mr. Howie, a Quaker. If the servants left the
cock of one of the barrels turned on he would
wedge himself into the hole to save the liquor.
Food had to be left out for him, and he punished
the cook if it was not good enough. The same
story is told of him as of the boggart in the Yorkshire tale, 'Aye, George, we're flitting'.

'CRODH MARA (Highland. Sea Cows). These are
harmless cattle belonging to the sea fairies, and
are sometimes given to human favourites.

COBLYNAU (The Welsh goblins). They are miners,
ugly to look at, but harmless and friendly to men.
They are about half a yard high and are dressed
like miners. Their presence brings good luck to
the mine, but they are rather formidable to meet
on their occasional holidays above-ground.

COLMAN GREY The name of a little fairy boy found
by a farmer. A story something like Skillywidden.

COLUINN GUN CHEANN (Highland. The Headless
Trunk). The name of a bauchan attached to the
Macdonalds of Morar. Though friendly to them,
he was very dangerous to the neighbourhood, as
he would attack and kill any single man who
passed by the River Morar after dark. He was at

length overcome and forced to leave those parts by one of the Macleods of Raasay.

THE COWIE   A spirit rather like a brownie. One haunted Goranberry Tower in the Border Country.

CWN ANNWN OR CWN Y WYBR   The Welsh hell hounds.

THE CYHYRAETH   (Welsh). The crying spirit. A kind of banshee, who wails before disasters.

THE DANA O'SHEE   (Ireland). These are the Heroic Fairies of Ireland, very like the Highland Sleeth Ma. May Eve — Beltane — and November Eve — Samhain — are their great festivals. On Beltane they revel, and — the door being open from fairyland to the mortal world that night — they often steal away beautiful mortals as their brides. On Samhain they dance with the ghosts. They live under fairy hills, offerings of milk are set out for them, and in all ways they partake of the fairy nature. Some say that they are fallen angels who were too good for hell and some that they are the remnants of the heroic Danaan race.

THE DERRICKS (Devon).   Ill-natured, dwarfish fairies.

THE DEVIL'S DANDY DOGS   (Cornwall). A pack of black hounds, fire-breathing and with fiery eyes, which the Devil leads over lonely moors on tempestuous nights. They will tear any living man to pieces, but they can be held off by the power of prayer.

THE DINNY MARA   The Manx Sea Man, mentioned by Campbell.

THE DOBBY   (Yorkshire), or Mr. Dobbs (Sussex). A brownie-like hobgoblin, who joins workmen and helps them at their task.

THE DOBIE   (Border Country). A rather clownish and foolish brownie. The dobie was sometimes invoked as the guardian of hidden treasure; but those who could get him preferred the cannier brownie as less likely to be outwitted. Ghosts are called dobies in Yorkshire.

THE DRACAE   Water Spirits. It was their custom to entice women to the water by appearing as wooden dishes floating down the stream. When a woman took hold of one it would resume its proper shape and drag her down into the water to nurse its children. Gervase of Tilbury tells a story of the dracae and a magic ointment, which is very like the Somerset story of 'The Fairy Midwife'.

THE DUERGAR   (Northumberland). A goblin race of fairies known on the Border, the worst and most malicious of the fairies.

DULLAHANS (Irish). Ghostly spirits like the headless woman who rode behind Larry Dodd in Crofton Croker's story.

THE DUNNIE (Northumberland). A kind of boggart, and like the Bogie Beast he was particularly fond of assuming the form of a horse. If a servant had hurriedly to ride for the midwife the dunnie would take a horse's form and let him down in a puddle or stream, and otherwise frighten and delay him. The dunnie seemed fond of water and craggy places, and used to sit hanging his legs over the crag at Hazelrig. Some think him the ghost of a reiver who died bearing a secret of undisclosed treasure, and so could not rest.

DUNTERS OR POWRIES (Scottish Border). These spirits inhabit old deserted peel towers and forts. They make a loud, constant noise like the beating of flax. If the noise becomes louder than usual it foretells a disaster.

EACH UISGE (Highland. The Water Horse). This horse is very much the same as the Kelpy, indeed so like it that there is much confusion between them. There are water horses in Ireland as well as in Scotland. In both countries they commonly took the form of handsome young men, who made love to maidens and then devoured them. They were to be detected by the sand and weed tangled in their hair.

THE ELLYLLDAN   The Welsh Will o' the Wisp.

THE ELLYLLON   The Welsh Elves. Tiny people, living on fairy butter (a kind of yellow fungus) and fairy food. Their Queen is Queen Mab.

ELVES   The Anglo-Saxon word for spirits of any kind, which later become specialized into creatures very like the Scandinavian Light Elves. Sir Walter Scott, in his *Demonology and Witchcraft*, describes elves as 'Sprites of a coarser sort, more laborious vocation and more malignant temper and in all respects less propitious to humanity than the Fairies.' This, however, applies only to the Scottish elves, and the little Scandinavian Light Elves, who looked after flowers, and whose chief faults were mischief and volatility, fit the general conception better. In Orkney and Shetland flint arrow heads are called Elf Shot, and are said to be fired by the trows, so that trow and elf seem synonymous terms with them.

FACHAN   (Highland).   A monster of the bodach type, with a tuft in the middle of his head and one hand coming out of his chest.

FEAR DEARG   (Irish. The Red Man).   A spirit known in Munster, whose visits brought good luck to a farm. He is described as a little man, about two and a half feet in height, dressed in a scarlet sugar loaf hat and a long scarlet cloak, with long grey hair and a wrinkled face. He would come in and ask to warm himself by the fire. It was very unlucky to refuse to let him in.

THE FERRIES An Orcadian name for fairies. They are gentler and more friendly and beautiful than the trows.

FERRIERS OR FERRISHERS A Suffolk name for fairies.

FETCH (Irish). The Irish name for a double of a living man, which was generally thought of as a death portent.

THE FIDEAL A malignant water spirit, like a girl in appearance, who haunts reedy lochs, and drags down and drowns swimmers. Loch na Fideal in Gairloch is named after her.

FIRBOLGS The Irish non-cannibal giants.

THE FOMORIANS The Scottish giants. They were great stone throwers, and nearly all the massy rocks scattered about Scotland would be somewhere else if it had not been for the fomorians. They bickered and squabbled among themselves, but are not as often accused of a liking for human flesh as are the English giants.

FUATH Pronounced foo-a. (Highland). The name of a whole class of malignant fairies or demons, Shellycoat, the Urisk, Each Uisge and others. Campbell, after giving some stories of them, says:

'From all these it appears that the Fuath in Sutherland is a water spirit, that there are males and females; that they have web feet, yellow hair, green dresses, tails, manes and no noses; that they marry men, and are killed by light, and hunt with steel weapons, and that in crossing a stream they become restless.'

GABRIEL HOUNDS OR RATCHETS The Gabriel hounds are like the wisht hounds, except that they hunt high in the air, and can be heard yelping overhead on stormy nights. To hear them is a presage of death. Some say that they are the souls of unchristened children, who can find no rest.

GALLY-TROT (Suffolk). A white dog, the size of a bullock, who pursues anyone who runs from it.

THE GANCONER (Irish. The Love-Talker). The love-talker strolls along lonely valleys with a pipe in his mouth, and makes love to young girls, who afterwards pine and die for him. In a story quoted in *Irish Fairy and Folk Tales* the ganconers appear in numbers, live in a city under a lough, hurl and play together, and steal human cattle, leaving a stock behind, just like ordinary Trooping Fairies.

GENTLE ANNIE (Cromarty Firth). A hag who raises and governs storms. Supposed to be of mild address and appearance, but treacherous and evil nature.

GHILLIE DHU (Highland. The Black Servant). A gentle-natured, solitary Fairy. He finds lost children and leads them home. His usual wear is tartan.

THE GENTRY The polite Irish name for fairies, equivalent to People of Peace; for it is not lucky to call them by their right name.

THE GLAISTIG (Highland). A female fairy, generally half woman, half goat, but sometimes described as a little, stout woman, clothed in green. She is a spirit of mixed characteristics, and seems, indeed, to be all fairies in little. She is supposed to be fond of children and the guardian of domestic animals. Milk is poured out to her, and she does something of a brownie's work about the house. She is specially kind, too, to old people and the feeble-minded. On the other hand she has darker qualities; there are stories of her misleading and slaying travellers. If the traveller named the weapon he had against her she could make it powerless; but if he only described it he could overcome her. The glaistig seems partly a water spirit. She might often be seen sitting by a stream, where she would beg to be carried across. She could be caught and set to work something like a kelpie.

THE GLASHTYN A Manx fairy, something after the style of Lob-Lie-by-the-Fire, though more sinister; for the story of the fuath who slept on the girl's knee is told about him, and a version of the Ainsel story.

THE GOOSEBERRY WIFE (Isle of Wight). A spirit, in the form of a large, hairy caterpillar, who looks after green gooseberries.

THE GRANT (English). A Demon, mentioned by Giraldus Cambrensis, very like the Picktree Brag. He is like a yearling colt in shape, but he goes on his hind legs and has fiery eyes. He is a town spirit, and runs down the middle of the street at midday or just after sundown, so that all the dogs run out barking. His appearance is a warning of danger. Some people connect him with Grendel, whom Beowulf killed; but Grendel was a sea monster.

GREMLINS The Air Force boggarts. It has been suggested that the name comes from the Anglo-Saxon gremian, to grieve, and has some distant connection with Grendel, the monster killed by Beowulf.

GRINDYLOW (Yorkshire). A malignant water demon.

THE GROGAN The Irish brownie, nearly related to the Highland gruagach.

THE GRUAGACH (Highland). A spirit with long, fair hair, who would often come drenched to the doors of the houses to beg for shelter. She was lucky about a house. A male gruagach is sometimes known. He wears a beaver hat and carries a wand. Like the brownie he is sometimes mischievous as well as helpful. Campbell mentions one that haunted Skipness Castle.

GUNNA (Highland) A solitary fairy, naked except for a fox-skin, who guards sheep-folds.

GWYN AP NUDD The Welsh King of the Fairies.

GWRAIG OR GWRAGEDD ANNWN (Welsh). Lake maidens, not unlike Malory's *Lady of the Lake*. They are beautiful, and not so dangerous as the mermaids and nixies. They have often wedded mortals.

GWRACH Y RHIBYN The Welsh banshee.

GWYDION The wizard king of the fairies of North Wales.

THE GWYLLION The hill fairies of Wales. Generally very forbidding and malignant. One of the commonest is the Old Woman of the Mountains, who leads night wanderers astray. A knife is a protection against them. The Gwyllion are close friends of the goats. They sometimes visit houses, where they must be hospitably entertained, or they will bring evil upon their hosts.

THE GYRE CARLING The name for the Fairy Queen in Fife.

HABETROT (Scottish Border). The spinning-wheel fairy. A shirt made by Habetrot was considered efficacious against many illnesses. Habetrot, though very ugly, was friendly to mankind.

THE HEDLEY KOW (Northumberland). A kind of bogie beast that haunted the village of Hedley. Its great amusement was to transform itself into one shape after another so as to bewilder whoever picked it up; but, like most spirits of its kind, it was fond of turning itself into a horse. Once it assumed the likeness of a pair of young girls, and led two young men into a bog. It is rare for a spirit to be able to make a double appearance.

HENKIES (Shetland and Orkneys). Trooping Fairies who limped as they danced. Their hills are called Henkie Knowes.

HOB OR HOBTHRUSH (Yorkshire and Durham). A hobgoblin with most of the usual brownie characteristics, but a specialist in whooping cough. Children with whooping cough used to be brought to Hobhole in Runswick Bay to be cured by Hob. The parents would call: 'Hobhole Hob! Hobhole Hob! My bairn's got kincough. Tak't off! Tak't off!' Like other brownies he is driven away by a present of clothes.

HOBYAHS A nasty swarm of malignant fairies, chiefly familiar through Jacob's story of 'Hobyah! Haob-yah!' They are very different from the generally harmless hobs. A dog is a great protection against them.

HOOKEYS A Lincolnshire name for fairies.

IMP Not really a fairy, only a small devil. Tom Tit
Tot is, however, called an impet.

INCUBUS More truly considered a demon than a fairy,
though Reginald Scot mentions him with the
brownie as having milk set out for him.

JEANNIE OF BIGGERSDALE (Yorkshire). A malignant
fairy, who lived in Mulgrave wood. Like a witch
she could not cross running water, and a young
farmer who rashly challenged her owed his life to
a stream.

JENNY GREENTEETH (Lancashire). A malignant water
fairy. She drags people down into the water and
drowns them. Her presence is indicated by a
green scum on the water.

THE KELPIE (Scottish). A malignant water spirit,
which is generally seen in the form of a horse, but
sometimes appears like a handsome young man.
A kelpie's great object is to induce mortals to
mount on its back and plunge with them into
deep water, where it devours them. A man who
can throw a bridle over the kelpie's head, however, has it in his power, and can force it to work
for him.

KILLMOULIS (Border Country). The Spirit of the
Mill. He is deeply attached to the miller's family,

but is often very mischievous and tiresome. He can sometimes, however, be persuaded to work at a pinch, and, like the brownie, he is often known to fetch the midwife for his mistress.

LEPRECHAUN (Irish). The fairy shoemaker. Keightley derives his name from Lubberkin, a variant of Lob.

THE LLAMHIGYN Y DWR (Welsh. The Water Leaper). A water spirit, who specially terrifies the fisherman, taking his bait and breaking the line. It drags sheep down into the water and feeds on them. Those who have hooked one say that it is rather like a toad with wings and a tail instead of legs. It gives such blood-curdling shrieks as it is dragged towards the shore that the fisherman is in danger of falling into the water and being sucked down.

LOB-LIE-BY-THE-FIRE Called the Lubbar Fiend by Milton. A hairy spirit with a long tail who labours hugely by night about the house which he haunts, and then lies by the fire to sleep. Like the brownie, he appreciates a bowl of milk.

THE LOIREAG (Highland). A water fairy, connected with fulling and weaving. She is described as 'a small scrap of womanhood that does not belong to this world', 'a plaintive little thing, stubborn and cunning'. She was fond of music, and was angry if any of the weavers sang out of tune.

LUBBERKIN An Elizabethan diminutive of lob, used for a puck-like fairy.

LURIDAN (Orkney). According to Reginald Scot Luridan was an Orcadian brownie, who inhabited the Island of Pomonia for some time. He swept and washed and lighted the fires in the mornings before the householders. This was the more remarkable, as he is elsewhere said to be the enemy of fire and to wage perpetual war against the Spirits of Fire. He announced to his friends that his time in Pomonia was short, for in seventy years he must give place to a mountain spirit called Balkin.

MAUG MOULACH OR HAIRY MEG (Highland). A spirit something between a brownie and a banshee. She haunts Tullochgorm and gives warning of the approaching death of any of the Grants. She also does brownie work. Maug Vlaucht, a spirit very like her, once haunted a Highland household with a companion called Brownie Clod.

MAUTHE DOOG (Isle of Man). The local name for the Black Dog which haunted the guard-room of Peel Castle.

MELCH DICK A wood spirit who protects unripe nuts.

THE MERMAID The mermaid is a much more sinister character than the mild roane, though harmless mermaids have been known. Her appearance and habits are well known to everyone from Scotland to Cornwall. It was considered a certain omen of shipwreck for a ship to sight a mermaid. The mermaids sometimes penetrated into rivers and sea lochs, as the story of 'The Mermaid of Knock-dolian' shows. In Suffolk, indeed, they are said to haunt ponds as well as rivers. Like many other fairies the mermaids have a great desire for human children. In the folk lore of a good many countries the mermaids and other water fairies are supposed to be very anxious to gain a human soul. Their lives are long, but when they die they perish utterly. (Such stories as the 'Legend of Undine' and the 'Little Mermaid' are built on this tradition.)

THE MERROWS The merrows are the Irish mer-people. Like the roane they live on dry land under the sea, and need an enchantment to make them able to pass through the water. The merrows' charm lies in their red caps. The merrows' women are very beautiful, but the men have long red noses, green teeth and hair and short finny arms.

THE MUILEARTACH (Highland). A giant hag with only one eye, so like the Cailleach Bheur as most probably to be only another name for her. She is specially connected with the sea, however, and occurs in several Fian legends.

NANCY BUTTONCAP (Yorkshire).
'The Moon shines bright,
The stars give light,
And little Nancy Buttoncap
Will come to-morrow night.'

NEAGLE, NOGGLE, NUGGLE OR NYAGGLE The Shetland water kelpie. He was like a horse, but his tail was shaped like the rim of a wheel, and he used it as a rudder in the water.

NUCKELAVEE (Scottish). A horrible monster who came out of the sea, half man and half horse, with a breath like pestilence and no skin on its body. The only security from it was that it could not face running water.

THE OLD LADY OF THE ELDER TREE (Lancashire). A tree spirit rather like Hans Andersen's 'Elder Flower Mother'.

OUPH An Elizabethan variant of elf.

PADFOOT A Yorkshire variant of the bogie beast. Generally described as the size of a donkey, black, shaggy and with fiery eyes. It follows people along dark roads at night. It can, however, take any shape, and often appears as a white dog. It gains its name from the sound of its feet, padding along beside the traveller in the darkness. Sometimes the rattling of a chain is heard too. Like the Black Dog it must not be spoken to or touched. It generally portends disaster.

THE PEALLAIDH (Highland). The Peallaidh or Shaggy One was said to be the chief of the Urisks. It lived in streams and amongst rocks. Its footprint is to be seen on a rock in Glen Lyon. Aberfeldy is said to be named after the Peallaidh. It is particularly at home in Perthshire.

PEERIFOOL (Shetland). The name of the fairy in the Shetland version of Tom Tit Tot. This story combines the plot of Fletcher's Bird with that of Tom Tit Tot. (See Orkney and Shetland Folk Lores.)

PEG O'NELL A spirit of the Ribble. Said to demand a life every seven years.

PEG POWLER The Spirit of the Tees. She has long green hair, and is insatiable for human life. The frothy foam on the higher reaches of the Tees is called Peg Powler's suds.

THE PEOPLE OF PEACE This is the Highland name for the fairies, corresponding to the Lowland Good Neighbours. They are much like them in character. Campbell's story of the 'Woman of Peace and the Kettle' is characteristic.

THE PELLINGS (Welsh. Rhys, *Celtic Folklore*). The Pellings of Corwrion Lake were a race of half fairies. Their mother was one of the Ladies of the Lake who had married a mortal and lived with him until he had accidentally touched her with cold iron. The pellings were held in such awe that parents would frighten their children into obedience with the mention of them. They gained their name from their mother, who was called Penelope.

PERRY DANCERS   This is the Suffolk name for Northern Lights, and is curiously like the Shetland peeries.

THE PHARISEES OR FRAIRIES   The Sussex, Suffolk, Warwickshire and Worcestershire name for fairies.

PHYNNODDEREE (or Fenodyree)   The Manx Brownie. The phynnodderee, like the brownie, works out doors and in, and, like the brownie, is rather touchy to deal with. There is a story of a phynnodderee whose farmer complained of his not cutting the corn near enough to the ground. He would mow no more, but next year followed the farmer, grubbing up the stubble so rapidly that he nearly cut off his legs. Like the brownie, the phynnodderee cannot be given clothing. This is his lament on finding clothes left for him:

> 'Cap for the head! Alas poor head!
> Coat for the back! Alas poor back!'

He is said to have been banished from the Fairy Court for the crime of dancing with a mortal maiden.

PICKTREE BRAG   This is a Durham version of the bogie beast. It appears in various forms, sometimes as a horse, sometimes as a calf or a dick ass, sometimes as a naked man without a head. It plays all the usual tricks of the bogie beast.

PINKET The Worcestershire name for the Will o' the Wisp.

PIXIES OR PISGIES (Devonshire and Cornwall). These are the small Trooping Fairies of which many stories are told by Hunt and Mrs. Bray. There are also occasional stories of the brownie type told of them. The white moths that come out in twilight are called pisgies in parts of Cornwall, and are regarded by some as fairies and by some as departed souls. In parts, too, they say that pixies are the spirits of unbaptized children.

THE PLANT RHYS DWFN (Welsh. Rhys, *Celtic Folklore*). A race of fairies, perhaps half human, on whose land there grows a plant which makes it invisible, and therefore impregnable. They used to come to the market in Cardigan and raise the prices of the corn and goods. Their invisible land is full of treasures. They are generally very honest, but have been known to steal babies.

THE PLANT ANNWN (Welsh). These are underwater fairies. They come up, dressed in green, to hunt lost souls with the Ban Hounds. Their milk-white cattle are a particularly fine breed. They are very like one race of the Tylwyth Teg.

THE PLENTYN-NEWID   The Welsh fairy changeling.

THE PORTUNES (English). These are a strange kind of fairy reported by Gervase of Tilbury and not surviving in any modern folk lore. They came in troops into farm houses at night, and, after working, rested themselves at the fire and cooked frogs for their supper. They were very tiny, with wrinkled faces and patched coats. It was in their nature to do good, not harm. Their only mischievous trick was that of misleading night horsemen.

POOKA (Irish). The Irish Puck is in many ways like the Dunnie or Brag. He is in appearance like a wild, shaggy colt, hung with chains. He generally haunts wild places, but in one story, though still keeping his animal form, he works like a brownie, and is stopped in his career of usefulness in the same way by the present of a coat. In this story, like the Cauld Lad, he is said to be the ghost of a servant.

PUCK A half domestic fairy, something between a brownie and a will o' the wisp. Shakespeare's Puck gives a good representation of him. The names Robin Goodfellow, Robin Hood and Hobgoblin seem to be indiscriminately applied to the same character.

PWCCA (Welsh). The Welsh puck is much the same character as in England and Ireland. He likes his nightly bowl of milk, but does not seem to work for it as the bwbachod do. He is specially fond of misleading night wanderers.

RAWHEAD-AND-BLOODY-BONES (Yorkshire, Lancashire and Lincolnshire). A malignant pond spirit who dragged children down into ponds and old marl pits. Sometimes called Tommy Rawhead.

REDCAP (The Border Country). A malignant spirit who haunts old peel towers and places where deeds of violence have been done. He is like a squat old man, with grim, long-nailed hands and a red cap, dyed in blood. It is dangerous to try to sleep in any ruined castle that he haunts, for if he can he will re-dip his cap in human blood. He can be driven off by words from Scripture or the sight of a cross-handled sword. In other places he is less sinister. There is, for instance, a Redcap who haunts Grandtully Castle in Perthshire, and who is rather lucky than unlucky.

THE ROANE or RON (The Highland Mermen). These mermen are distinguished from others by travelling through the sea in the form of seals. In the depths of the sea caves they come to air again, and there and on land they cast off the seal skins which are necessary to carry them through water. The roane are peculiarly mild unrevengeful fairies of deep domestic affections, as the stories of 'The Fisherman and Merman' and 'The Seal Catcher's Adventure' show. The Shetlanders call the roane

Sea Trows, but their character is substantially the same.

ROBIN GOODFELLOW (English). This is one of the Elizabethan names for Puck; but whether it had existed long or had been invented by the unknown author of *The Merry Jests of Robin Goodfellow*, printed about 1584, it is now difficult to decide. Robin Goodfellow in this book is said to be the child of a marriage between a mortal and a fairy; all the regular fairy activities are ascribed to him. He turned himself into a horse and dropped his rider into water, he worked for a farm servant but was laid by a suit of clothes, he misled travellers as a Willy Wisp. Reginald Scot gives much the same account of him, and so does Burton.

ROBIN ROUNDCAP An East Yorkshire brownie.

THE SEELY COURT (Lowland Scots). Seely means blessed, and this name stands for the comparatively virtuous Heroic Fairies. The malignant fairies and demons were sometimes called the Unseely Court.

THE SELKIE OR SILKIE The seal men of the Orkneys. Orkney and Shetland folk lore gives one or two interesting stories of the selkies, particularly the long and unusual ballad of 'Lady Odivere and the Selkie'.

SHAG, SHAGFOAL OR TATTERFOAL The Lincolnshire

version of a brag. Its appearance is sufficiently described by its name.

SHELLYCOAT (Scottish). A mischievous bogle, dressed in water weed and shells, whose clinking tells us who he is. Like the brag he delights in misleading night wanderers. He specially haunts the old house of Gorrinberry in Liddesdale, and there was also a fierce Shellycoat near Leith.

SHEFRO (Irish). A gregarious fairy, who, according to Hartley Coleridge, wears foxglove heads for caps.

THE SHOCK (Suffolk). The Suffolk brag.

SILI-GO-DWT AND SILI FFRIT Names of little Welsh fairies, something of the kind of the Scottish Whuppity Stoorie.

SHONY (Scottish). The Spirit of the Sea on the West Coast of Scotland.

SHOOPILTEE (Shetland). This is the Shetland water kelpie. He appears as a pretty little horse; but when people mount him he gallops off with them into the sea and drowns them.

SHRIKER (Yorkshire and Lancashire). A death portent. Sometimes it is called a brash, from the padding of its feet. It sometimes wanders invisibly in the woods, giving fearful shrieks, and at others it takes a form like padfoot, a large dog with huge feet and saucer eyes.

SILKY (Northern Counties). A name for a white lady. The Silky of Black Heddon in Northumberland had one close resemblance to a brownie. If she found things below stairs untidy at night she would tidy them, but if they had been tidied she flung them about. She was dressed in dazzling silks, and went about near the house, swinging herself in Silky's Chair — the crossed branches of an old tree which overhangs a waterfall — riding sometimes behind horsemen or stopping them by standing in front of their horses. But on the whole perhaps she belonged more to the class of ghosts than of brownies, for she was laid by the discovery of a treasure, which must have been troubling her.

SKILLYWIDDEN (English). The name of a little fairy boy found sleeping and carried home by a farmer in Treridge.

SLEAGH MAITH (Highland). The Good People, described by Kirke.

THE SPRIGGANS (Cornwall). Some say the spriggans are the ghosts of the giants. They haunt old cromlechs and standing stones and guard their buried treasure. They are grotesque in shape, with the power of swelling from small into monstrous size. For all commotions and disturbances in the air, mysterious destruction of buildings or cattle, loss of children or the substitution of changelings, the spriggans may be blamed.

SPOTLOGGIN The ghost of a murdered man who haunts a ditch near Evesham. On the spot where the murder took place no hedge is supposed to grow.

SWARTH Cumberland name for fetch or double.

TANGIE (Orkneys). Tangie is the water kelpie of the Orkneys. He is named from the tang, or seaweed, which covers him. He appears sometimes as a man and sometimes as a horse, like each uisge.

TANTERABOGUS (Somerset and Devon). A bogie who comes after bad children.

TARANS (Scottish). The spirits of unbaptized children are called tarans in the north-east of Scotland.

THRUMMY CAP (Border). A spirit who haunted the cellars of old houses. He wore a cap made out of weavers' thrums.

THRUMPIN A familiar demon, believed by the Border people to haunt every man and to have the power of taking away his life.

TROWS (Orkney, Shetland and wherever Scandinavian blood is found). In *Scottish Fairy and Folk Tales* the Shetland story of 'Thom and Willie' gives some idea of the habits and appearance of the trows. They are called the Grey People, are small, have a Queen and dine daintily but lavishly off gold and silver plate. They ride bulrushes. Like all the Trooping Fairies they steal children and lying-in mothers, and are great thieves of milk and cattle. They possess many infallible remedies, which they often bestow on their mortal favourites. The Folk Lore of Orkney gives a good story of 'The Day Bound Trow'.

TRWTYN-TRATYN   The Welsh Tom Tit Tot.

TOM DOCKIN   (North of England).   A bogie with iron teeth, who devours bad children.

TOM POKER   (East Anglia).   A bogie who inhabits dark closets, holes under stairs and cocklofts.

TOM TIT TOT   (Suffolk).   The English Rumpel-stiltzkin. He is described as a black thing with a long tail, and sometimes as an impet. Tom-Tit, a Tut or a Tut-gut is a Lincolnshire name for a hobgoblin.

TOD LOWREY   The Scottish name for a fox, is used in Lincolnshire for a kind of hobgoblin.

THE TYLWYTH TEG, OR FAIR FAMILY   (Wales).   It is difficult to get a clear picture of the tylwyth teg. The name is very much used, and for differing types of fairies. They are sometimes described as of mortal or more than mortal size, dressed chiefly in white. They live on an invisible island; they

223

ride about hunting and reward cleanliness with
gifts of money; they dance in fairy rings, and
mortals joining them are made invisible and
carried off for ever, unless they are rescued before
cockcrow. Others wear rayed clothes of green and
yellow, are small and thieving, particularly of milk
and human children. Unlike many fairies the
tylwyth teg are golden haired and will only show
themselves to fair-haired people. The usual
brownie story is also told about them. They are
very friendly with the goats, and comb their
beards for Sundays.

Urchin   Urchin, the popular name for hedgehog, was
used in the sixteenth century and earlier for a
rather pixie-like fairy. Reginald Scot mentions it
in his list of fairies, and so does Shakespeare and
Ben Jonson, but it is not, so far as I know, used
traditionally for any fairy in any dialect.

The Urisk   (Highland). A kind of rough brownie,
half human and half goat, very lucky to have
about the house, who herded the cattle and
worked on farms. He haunted lonely waterfalls,
but would often crave human company, and
follow terrified travellers at night, without, however, doing them any harm. The urisks lived
solitary in recesses of the hills, but they would
meet at stated times for solemn assemblies. A
corrie near Loch Katrine was their favourite
meeting place.

VOUGHA Another name for the fuath, the malignant Highland water spirits.

WAFF Yorkshire for fetch.

WAG-AT-THE-WA' (Scottish Border). This spirit, though domestic and friendly to the family, was much dreaded in the Border Country, and it was considered unchancy to swing the pot hook hanging from the chimney when it was empty, for it was an invitation to the Wag-at-the-Wa' to sit there.

WATER WRAITH The Scottish female water spirit. Dressed in green, withered, meagre and scowling.

WEREWOLF The werewolf, or human in wolf's form, died out of Britain with the wolves.

WHUPPITY STOORIE A Scottish female Rumpelstiltzkin.

WILKIE (Orkney and Shetland). The Shetland name for a fairy. It is possible that Wilkie Howe, the name of a fairy hill in the East Riding of Yorkshire may be an example of the same name, for there is a common Scandinavian origin.

WILL O' THE WISP The commonest name for the Ignis fatuus.

THE WISHT HOUNDS OR YETH HOUNDS (Somerset, Devon and Cornwall). A phantom pack of hounds breathing flames, who hunt about the heaths for lost souls or living men with the devil as their huntsman.

WRYNECK (Lancashire). A malignant spirit. 'He caps Wryneck, and Wryneck caps the Dule.'

YALLERY BROWN (West of England). The name of a small impet so malignant that it was dangerous to earn even his gratitude. His story is told by Jacobs in *More English Fairy Tales*.

A LIST OF SELECTED BOOKS

SOURCES OF STORIES SUITABLE FOR TELLING

Annals of King Oberon. Everyman Library.

CAMPBELL, J. F. *Popular Tales of the Western Highlands.* Alexander Gardner.

CHAMBERS, R. *Popular Rhymes of Scotland.* Chambers.

CROKER, C. *Fairy Legends and Traditions of the South of Ireland.* John Murray.

DOUGLAS, G. *Scottish Fairy and Folk Tales.* Scott Publishing Library.

Fairy Gold. Everyman Library.

GUEST, C. *The Mabinogian.* Everyman Library.

HARTLAND, E. S. *English Fairy and Folk Tales.* Scott Publishing Library.

HUNT, R. *Popular Romances of the West of England.* Chatto & Windus.

JACOBS, J. *English Fairy Tales.* D. Nutt.
   More English Fairy Tales.
   Celtic Fairy Tales.
   More Celtic Fairy Tales.

KEIGHTLEY, T. *Fairy Mythology.* Bohn Library.

KENNEDY, P. *Legendary Fictions of the Irish Celts.* Macmillan.

O'GRADY, S. H. *Silva Gadelica.* Williams & Norgate.

HALLIWELL-PHILLIPPS, J. O. *Nursery Rhymes and Nursery Tales of England.* Frederick Warne.

RITSON, J. *Fairy Tales.* Payne & Foss.

ROLLESTON, T. W. *Myths and Legends of the Celtic Race.* Harrap.

WILDE, F. S. *Ancient Legends of Ireland.* Ward & Downey.

YEATS, W. B. *Irish Fairy and Folk Tales.* Scott Publishing Library.

THE PERSONNEL OF FAIRYLAND

BOOKS ON FAIRY LORE

ALLIES, J. *Folk Lore of Worcestershire.* Folk-Lore Society.

BARING GOULD, S. *A Book of Folk Lore.* Collins.

BURNE, C. S. & JACKSON, G. *Shropshire Folk-Lore.* Trübner.

CLODD, E. *Tom Tit Tot.* Duckworth.

County Folk-Lore. Various Counties. Folk-Lore Society.

HARLAND AND WILKINSON. *Lancashire Folk-Lore.* John Heywood.

HENDERSON, W. *Folk-Lore of the Northern Counties of England and the Borders.* Folk-Lore Society.

KIRKE, R. *The Secret Commonwealth.* Mackay.

MACKENZIE, D. *Scottish Folk-Lore and Folk Life.* Blackie.

MACPHERSON, J. M. *Primitive Beliefs in the North East of Scotland.* Longmans.

MILLER, H. *The Old Red Sandstone.* Everyman Library.

RHYS, E. *Celtic Folklore, Welsh and Manx.* Oxford University Press.

SCOTT, W. *Demonology and Witchcraft.* Oliver & Boyd.
Minstrelsy of the Scottish Border. Blackwood.

SIKES, W. *British Goblins.* Sampson Low.

SPENCE, J. E. *Shetland Folk-Lore.* Johnson & Greig.

WENTZ, E. *The Fairy Faith in Celtic Countries.* Oxford University Press.

WRIGHT, E. M. *Rustic Speech and Folk-Lore.* Oxford University Press.